Cheers to TV

Cocktails Inspired by
Iconic Television Characters

Will Francis
Illustrated by Stacey Marsh

Prestel

Munich · London · New York

Cocktails

Introduction

Cocktails have long played a role in popular culture–books, music, film, and TV. Sure, a cocktail is just some alcohol, juice, sugar, and the like all shaken up with ice. Yet the sum total of these exotic liquids, gathered from around the globe and assembled in a glass, seems to amount to something more.

Take the Old Fashioned, for instance: a very simple drink comprising whiskey, sugar, bitters, and orange zest. But to have one made for you by an expert bartender, to see the precision of the build, the care and patience in stirring, cooling, diluting, the garnish of zest being carefully cut, rubbed around the glass, mounted on the rim and then passed over the bar to you: it feels special and worthy of reverence, even though it's only a mere bit of a drink to be slurped away.

And so, these characterful little concoctions have come to take on cultural significance over the 150 years or so in which mixology has existed in its current form. Flamboyant but relaxed Gin Rickeys typified the roaring 1920s. Sweet Tiki-style drinks such as the Mai Tai and Zombie exploded into popular culture in the 1960s, while the 1980s saw spring break hits like Sex on the Beach dial up the fun factor.

Then, in more recent years, as society has turned increasingly retrospective (every new trend seems like a reference to a previous decade now), mixology has become far more heritage-focused. The way that bars and bartenders are presented tends to be more traditional, and menus are bringing back classics from those earlier days of creating cocktails. Sweet crowd-pleasers like Mojitos and Cosmopolitans have been making way for more refined drinks like Martinis and Negronis, as palates once again lean toward more bitter and alcohol-heavy notes.

In our previous book, *Cocktails of the Movies*, we charted the intertwined history of mixed drinks and film, and how the two reflected wider cultural changes over the last century. But while the cinematic format has remained largely unchanged, television–which we focus on here–has been on much more of a journey of constant iteration and innovation.

Aside from the rise of reality TV and rolling news in recent decades, the other major shift has been seen in fictional drama, thrillers, and comedies. The most noticeable difference between what's on the small screen today and what twentieth-century audiences had access to is the sheer complexity of these pieces. TV is pricier to produce than ever, but also requires much more time and attention from the viewer.

This growing ambition of the format has partly been due to the rise of home video, physical box sets, and other on-demand options. While a show like the seminal 2000s thriller *24* would air live on cable television every week, it could also be bought by the season on DVD, with viewers able to binge-watch at their leisure without missing a vital scene. Fast forward to today, and we have immediate access to everything all the time, meaning narratives can be more involved and complex than ever before, simply because we can consume them as we please.

It has been said many times over the last decade that serial television is going through a golden age, with TV seemingly at its peak quality. A big driver of this is the massive budgets being wielded by tech companies such as Netflix, Amazon, and Apple, who seek to acquire "users" for their streaming platforms. Not long ago, the

Gibson - page 66

stars of Hollywood would view a TV role as a low point, an admission that they desperately needed work. Nowadays, some of the most captivating, textured, and interesting characters are explored in multi-season television shows. Those roles are now sought after as opportunities to demonstrate one's acting craft and delve deeper into a character's portrayal over the course of several seasons, as well as to garner that all-important critical acclaim.

Just as in the movies, cocktails have been used as a way to say something about a character on the small screen too, a subtle motif to hint at their inner life. In this book we feature 60 such drinks that are consumed by, or inspired by, a wide range of characters. In *The Queen's Gambit*, Beth's adoptive mother drinks Gibsons, and after her passing Beth does too. The drink is cold and dry, much like the two women's relationship with one another. It's also a strong tipple, used as a crutch by a steely but inwardly vulnerable character. Conversely, in *Scrubs*, we regularly see J.D. order his favorite drink, the Appletini. He's a goofy kind of guy who doesn't care much what people think, and despite the fact that ordering this drink invariably makes situations awkward, he loves it with endearingly non-ironic glee.

Then there are drinks that some of our most beloved characters invent right there on a show. Patsy of *Absolutely Fabulous* gave us the Stoli-Bolli, a straight-to-the-point concoction of premium liquids. But many cocktails born on screen are a little more offbeat, and in sharing recipes for these here we've taken creative license. Super Fight Milk from *It's Always Sunny in Philadelphia* should apparently be made with crow's eggs, milk, and vodka, so we've turned that into an equally protein-heavy but far nicer eggnog-style affair. Michael Scott's dangerous-sounding One of Everything from *The Office* needed tweaking to become something akin to a Long Island Iced Tea (and no, the Splenda didn't make the final recipe). And then there's

Liz Lemon's Funky Juice from *30 Rock*, which is just white wine and Sprite, and it turns out … that's actually a great recipe, with a bit of attention to proportions and serving. Just don't keep it in a flask next to the toilet, as Liz does.

We've also included tribute drinks, which make up over half of the cocktails featured in this book; they're here to celebrate something essential in the associated show. These are a blend of original creations concocted by us along with existing recipes sourced from the annals of mixology that speak to a particular character's traits.

It's a mammoth undertaking to dive into hundreds of classic movies to seek out dozens of unique, good drinks featured somewhere

within. While we're proud of the results in *Cocktails of the Movies*, the process with this book has been very different. Unfettered by historical facts, we've enjoyed the freedom to include cocktails here that are lesser-known but that, in our opinion, everyone should try making, or ordering.

The Penicillin, for instance, which we present to celebrate the Y2K-era medical drama *ER*, is a whiskey-lover's dream and a recognized modern classic that fuses honey, ginger, and two different whiskies. The Bed & Breakfast Martini, a riff on a gin and orange ordered at Fawlty Towers, is our take on the iconic Martini, but with a very orangey twist, thanks largely to the inclusion of marmalade. If you've only tried this citrus preserve on toast, you're missing out. Paired with gin (as here) or tequila, it's a fantastically bittersweet cocktail ingredient.

Whichever page you find yourself on, you'll surely find something interesting to drink and to watch. Whatever you create, just remember that if it tastes good, it's perfect. Whether you used the exact recipe proportions, utilized the proper gear, or served it in the right glass is all mere detail in the bigger picture of you and your guests enjoying a drink—and, more importantly, a convivial moment—together.

Bar Equipment

The essential tools of mixology

You don't need lots of elaborate gear to get started making good cocktails–it is, after all, the ingredients that really count. Here's a starter set of basic tools that will allow you to create just about any recipe you find in this book or elsewhere.

Shaker

Choose between the Boston and Cobbler shaker. The former is simply a large, sturdy glass with a slightly larger steel cup. The latter is a three-piece cup, lid, and strainer assembly which, while popular in home bars due to its aesthetic appeal, is in fact less practical and unpopular with professional bartenders. We recommend a Boston set as it is easier to clean, quicker to use, and handy for stirred cocktails too.

Muddler

Fruit and herbs often need to be muddled with sugar or liquor in the bottom of your mixing glass to release their juices, oils, and flavors. Use an unvarnished wooden muddler for gently pressing mint and similar leaves. A steel muddler with raised teeth at one end is best for muddling fruit. Take care not to over-muddle your ingredients as this can leave your cocktail tasting bitter, as well as filling it with a multitude of annoying bits.

Jigger

Measuring your cocktail ingredients accurately is crucial not just for making great drinks, but for testing new recipes, refining them, and creating your own. A standard steel jigger usually holds 1 shot (1 oz / 30 ml) in the small end and 2 shots (2 oz / 60 ml) in the large end.

Hawthorne Strainer

An essential item if you're using a Boston shaker set, the Hawthorne strainer is a flat, perforated steel paddle with a wire spring around its edge which fits the end of your Boston tin, keeping fruit pieces and ice in while you pour your shaken or stirred cocktail out. It lets out smaller ice shards that have broken up during shaking, as well as some fruit pulp, which is fine for most cocktails served over ice.

Fine Strainer

For Martinis and the like, which are served without ice in a chilled glass, you'll need to fine strain to avoid fruit pulp and small ice fragments collecting on the surface and spoiling the elegance of your carefully crafted drink. A good fine strainer keeps all these bits out while not getting so clogged up that it stops the drink flowing through into your serving glass.

Bar Spoon

The unsung hero of the mixologist's toolkit is the traditional bar spoon. With its long, twisted stem joining a flat disc at one end and its large teaspoon at the other, it is indispensable for stirring, layering and measuring syrups, scooping Maraschino cherries from jars, and generally making life easier for every bartender. Its flat end can even be used to muddle, though you will find this much easier with the aforementioned muddler.

Base Spirits

The leading lights of your cocktail cabinet

These are the six base spirits on which almost all alcoholic cocktails are built. As a rule, the darker the spirit, the longer it has been barrel-aged, and the deeper the flavor.

Gin

Arguably the most important spirit in your cocktail cabinet, and in the history of mixed drinks, gin is the star of many classics from sweet Martinis to bitter Negronis. To make it, grain alcohol is distilled and/ or steeped with botanicals including the traditional juniper berry, together with anything from orange zest to cinnamon to cucumber, to create a unique flavor profile. London gin is dry, while the less common Old Tom gin is sweet. Sloe gin is a berry liqueur made with gin.

Whiskey

Whiskey has arguably become a family of spirits, with Scotch, Irish, bourbon, and rye the most popular members. They are all distilled from grain mash and aged in wooden casks, with locally available grains and wood determining their distinct flavors. Generally speaking, Scotch whisky is made with peat-smoked malt, Irish with unpeated malt, bourbon with corn (maize), and rye with rye. All must meet minimum cask-aging requirements if they are legally to bear their name.

Vodka

By far the most neutral spirit, vodka is almost solely pure alcohol (ethanol) and water. It is distilled from starchy foods such as oats, rye, barley, wheat, and potatoes. Given vodka's lack of flavor, it is highly useful for giving a kick to already-rich flavor combinations without interfering with the taste. You can even make your own gin by infusing a good vodka with your own blend of botanicals.

Brandy

Made from distilled wine, brandy is often drunk on its own and is best consumed at room temperature or slightly warm. It works particularly well in hot cocktails and desserts, to which it adds a beautifully rounded warmth. The most common variety is cognac, which must be from the wine-producing area around the town of the same name, twice-distilled in copper pot stills, and aged for two years in special French oak barrels.

Rum

Distilled from molasses, a byproduct of refined sugar, most rums come from the Caribbean and Latin America. At one end of the scale is light rum, typically from Cuba and Puerto Rico, and at the other are the dark rums of Jamaica, which are distilled and aged for longer. In between are a myriad of grades from all over the region and indeed the world. Light rum is the most mixable and is well suited to cocktails, forming the basis of such classics as the Daiquiri and the Mojito.

Tequila

Distilled from the huge piñas of the blue agave plant, some form of tequila appears to have been around for hundreds and perhaps even thousands of years. It was originally enjoyed by the Aztec people of Mexico, and subsequently by the Spanish conquistadors, who started to produce their own take on it in the sixteenth century. It enjoys unprecedented popularity today, with a growing number of high-quality brands becoming widely available.

Liqueurs, Juices, and Bitters

Building blocks with a million combinations

The combinations really do become endless when these building blocks enter the mix. From fruit and nut liqueurs to botanical bitters and juices, there is infinite creative scope here.

Vermouth and Aperitifs

Vermouth has been a staple of the cocktail bar for 200 years, bringing its botanical flavors to classics like the Martini, Manhattan, and Negroni. The name of this fortified wine originates from the German word for wormwood–*Wermut*–as this has always been a key botanical used to aromatize the base wine, and was once believed to have medicinal value. French vermouth is white and usually dry, while Italian vermouth is red and usually sweet.

Liqueurs

Bold fruit, nut, and other natural flavors are commonly brought to a cocktail through sweet liqueurs such as Cointreau (orange), crème de cassis (blackcurrant), or Frangelico (hazelnut). It is important to use liqueurs with caution as it tends to be easier to oversweeten a drink than it is to oversour it. Oversweetening can also be hard to undo. Overall, orange liqueur–also known as triple sec or the slightly sweeter curaçao–is the liqueur used most often in this book.

Bitters

Originally created as medicines for minor ailments, bitters are highly concentrated blends of alcohol, water, and botanical extracts that have become indispensable to the modern bartender. The most famous bitters are those by Angostura, for which only very few people know the closely guarded recipe. Other useful types to stock are orange bitters and Peychaud's bitters. Today, there are a growing number of bartenders infusing their own unique flavors.

Fruit Juice

Always squeeze your own citrus juice. You'll usually need the zest or a slice of it for garnish anyway, and bottled citrus juice is no replacement. Other juices can be impractical to squeeze yourself and are used less often, so buy multipacks of single-serving cartons of juices such as cranberry, pineapple, and apple to ensure you always have a constant supply.

Sugar Syrup

Most cocktails require added sweetness, usually in the form of sugar syrup (also called "simple syrup." Buy it in bottles or make your own by adding two parts sugar to one part hot (not boiling) water in a pan. Stir over a gentle heat, making sure not to boil or caramelize the sugar, until dissolved, and pour into a bottle that has been rinsed with a shot of vodka. If you prefer to avoid refined sugar, you can use agave syrup in cocktails where its more amber color and flavor are welcome.

Eggs and Milk

Some people are uncomfortable with consuming uncooked eggs, though if they are from free-range, organic farms the risk of illness is remote. The mouthfeel and flavor that egg whites bring to a drink are unique, and powdered egg whites are available for those not comfortable with fresh. Milk and cream can equally make for a fine cocktail, from "hard shakes" to the classic White Russian.

Garnishes

Turning a mere mixed drink into a fine cocktail

Just as we "eat with our eyes," so we drink with them too. A cocktail's appeal is multiplied with artful presentation, and the key elements listed below are used throughout this book. Prepare your garnishes first so they will be ready as soon as your drink is mixed, ensuring optimal freshness.

Citrus Twists

Use a vegetable peeler or small knife to take a wide strip of skin from the fruit, without including too much of the bitter pith. The oils from this are usually expressed into a drink to give extra flavor and aroma by folding it over the drink and wiping around the rim. Thin twists, which are more for decoration, are created with a channel knife. These can then be wrapped around a straw to set them in a helix shape before being draped over the glass rim.

Flamed Zest

This technique adds a more complex flavor and aroma to the right drink, and a little fiery theater to your cocktail preparation. Try it with a Cosmopolitan or an Old Fashioned. Skim a disc of skin from the fruit—usually an orange—and set aside while you light your match. Allow the phosphorus to burn off and the flame to settle down. Hold the flame above but not directly over the glass, and express the oil from the zest through the flame and onto your drink.

Ice

You'll need ice for almost every cocktail, to both cool and dilute a drink as you shake or stir. It is best to either buy large bags made with mineral water from the supermarket, or freeze your own cubes with water from a filtering tap or jug.

An ice crusher is handy, though you can crush ice for drinks such as Mint Juleps and Daiquiris simply by wrapping cubes in a clean dish towel and bashing with your muddler.

Skewered Fruit

Cherries, fruit slices, and leaves can be combined in a million ways on a cocktail stick for extra dramatic effect when serving mixed drinks. They can be skewered like a kebob and rested between the sides of the glass, attached to a fruit wedge mounted on the rim, or even balanced on a floating hollow "boat" made from a juiced lime skin or a halved and scooped-out passionfruit.

Rim Dusting

Dusting a rim with salt, sweet, or sour powder can add visual appeal and complementary flavors. To salt a Margarita rim, prepare your lime slice garnish and wipe round the rim to moisten it before tamping the glass upside down in a saucer of salt. This technique can be used for cocoa (with orange), cinnamon (with apple), and many other flavor combinations.

Umbrellas, Straws, and Sticks

Many cocktail aficionados disapprove of the use of umbrellas, believing they undermine the seriousness of refined drinking. There are some drinks, however, such as the Banana Daiquiri and the Singapore Sling, which somehow require a touch of flamboyant color to complete the tropical theme. Keep a stock of standard cocktail sticks and straws (long and short), but don't be afraid to pick up novelty variants when you see them, as guests will love them.

Glassware

Setting the stage for a star turn

To make the cocktails in this book, and all well-known ones, you'll need the glasses shown here. You can however make the majority of cocktails if, to begin with, you have only the first four.

MARTINI
GLASS

CHAMPAGNE
FLUTE

COLLINS
GLASS

ROCKS
GLASS

OLD FASHIONED GLASS

COUPE

RED WINE GLASS

COPPER MULE MUG

MARGARITA GLASS

HIGHBALL GLASS

HURRICANE GLASS

SHOT GLASS

TIKI MUG

19th Century

QUANTUM LEAP
SAM BECKETT | SCOTT BAKULA
SCIENCE FICTION • USA • 1989

Trapped in time due to an experiment gone wrong, former scientist Dr. Sam Beckett (played by Scott Bakula) jumps into the body of a different person during every episode of *Quantum Leap*.

The show kicks off when, after being pressured by the threat of loss of government funding for his time-travel project, codenamed "Quantum Leap," Sam decides to hop in the nuclear accelerator early and instantly disappears into the past. He eventually wakes up to discover that he is now an Air Force test pilot named Tom Stratton, but has little recollection of his former life—he can't remember his last name and doesn't even recognize his own face in the mirror.

Al, a friend from Sam's own time, shows up in the form of a hologram that only Sam can see and hear. It is Al who informs Sam that his project hasn't panned out how they had hoped, and now he must put right all the wrongs in the life of Tom Stratton in order to leap home. Sam succeeds, but keeps randomly leaping into different bodies, correcting the past and hoping that, maybe this time, he'll end up where he started—but will he ever get back?

....

1½ shots bourbon

¾ shot crème de cacao

¾ shot Lillet Rouge

¾ shot fresh lemon juice

Shake all ingredients with ice, and fine strain into a chilled coupe glass.

In the late 1930s, a bartender at the Piccadilly Hotel in London, C. A. Tuck, created the 20th Century cocktail. The drink grew popular, and came to be associated with luxury travel since it was named after the most famous train in America at the time. Fast forward to 2016, and its unique flavor combination enjoyed a revival thanks to Brian Miller at New York's Pegu Club, who created the 19th Century—a twist on the original, substituting gin with bourbon.

This heritage-style cocktail will transport you back to those early days of bartending, with ingredients popular at the time and a serve style that would be at home in any fin-de-siècle hotel.

THE X-FILES
DANA SCULLY | GILLIAN ANDERSON
SCIENCE FICTION • USA • 1993

2 shots Absolut Mandarin Vodka

½ shot blue curaçao

1 shot cranberry juice

¼ shot fresh lime juice

½ shot sour mix

Shake all ingredients with ice, and strain into a Collins glass filled with crushed ice.

Delve into the strange and inexplicable world of *The X-Files*, a cult classic TV show which earned its status as a pop culture icon over the course of 11 seasons.

The show follows the investigations of FBI agent Fox Mulder (David Duchovny), a cunning profiler and adamant believer in the supernatural and extra-terrestrial life, who is tasked with solving a spate of seemingly mystifying cases. Joining him is medical doctor and ardent skeptic Dana Scully, played by Gillian Anderson.

Scully first encounters Mulder in the dank basement of an FBI building, having been assigned to assist "Spooky Mulder" (as he has come to be known by his colleagues) with the unsolved X-Files. Opposed to any notion of the paranormal, she is always the voice of reason.

Mulder refuses to give in to Scully's cold, scientific explanations as the two go on a number of nationwide investigations into increasingly bizarre crime cases. The truth is out there, and they're determined to uncover it.

This cocktail was created exclusively for the wrap party for what was believed at the time to be the last ever episode of the show. The event took place at House of Blues in Los Angeles in 2002, with 1,200 past and present crew and cast members partying into the wee hours. There was a menu of drinks sponsored by the Swedish vodka brand Absolut. However, this particular cocktail seems to have broken out into the wider fandom of "X-Philes," and rightly so—it's a tasty tipple that is essentially a colorful, sweet twist on the classic Cosmopolitan.

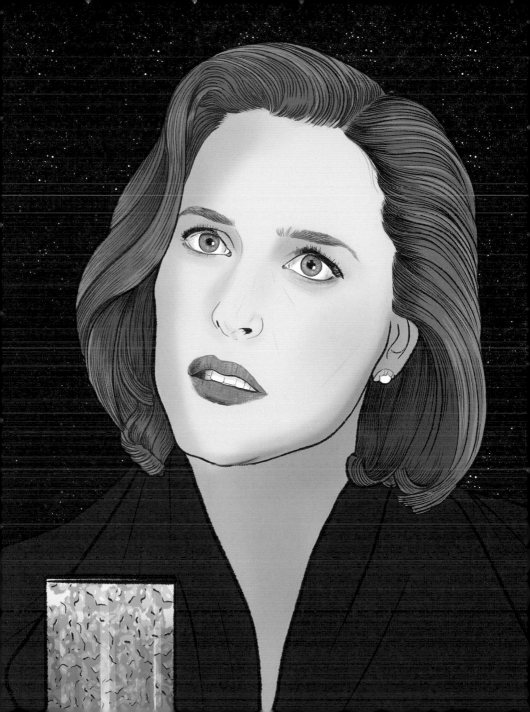

BREAKING BAD
WALTER WHITE | BRYAN CRANSTON
CRIME DRAMA • USA • 2008

Set in Albuquerque, New Mexico, between 2008 and 2010, *Breaking Bad* follows Walter White (Bryan Cranston), a high-school chemistry teacher who becomes a ruthless participant in the local methamphetamine drug trade. Walter's drastic change in career stems from his desire to financially provide for his family after he is diagnosed with terminal lung cancer.

The psychological complexities of Walter's character are apparent from the offset: he's both a merciless and egotistical dealer working with Mexican drug cartels, and a cheated family man who is staring death in the face. But it is Walter and his former student Jesse Pinkman's heart-breaking partners-in-crime relationship which really keeps audiences fully invested. Jesse (played by Aaron Paul) transforms during the show, from a reckless addict to a more caring man who is able to manage his emotions, while Walter furthers his career in crime and drugs.

. . . .

A lighter-flavored take on the classic Long Island Iced Tea, this long-popular variation packs no less of a punch. In bright blue, it looks just like the meth that Walter cooks up in his lab–and, similarly, should be approached with caution.

Its origins are vague, but by all accounts this drink seems to have emerged in 1980s America. It's not hard to imagine it evolving out of spring break parties and clubs, given its high alcohol content and fun color scheme. But if you think it's a cheap thrill, think again. Much like its cola-based cousin, this is a surprisingly tasty beverage whose place at the bar is well deserved.

½ **shot** vodka

½ **shot** rum

½ **shot** tequila

½ **shot** gin

½ **shot** blue curaçao

½ **shot** fresh lemon juice

½ **shot** fresh lime juice

½ **shot** sugar syrup

Lemon-limeade, such as Sprite or 7UP, to top

Garnish: lemon and cocktail cherry sail

Shake all ingredients except the lemon-limeade together with ice, and strain into an ice-filled Collins glass. Top with the lemon-limeade and garnish.

Aguardiente Sour

2 shots aguardiente

¾ shot fresh lemon juice

¾ shot sugar syrup

½ egg white, lightly beaten

Garnish: lemon slice

Shake all ingredients vigorously without ice for 30 seconds, then with ice for another 30. Strain into an ice-filled Old Fashioned glass and garnish.

MODERN FAMILY
GLORIA DELGADO-PRITCHETT | SOFIA VERGARA
SITCOM • USA • 2009

This show revolves around three families living in Los Angeles who are all interrelated through Jay Pritchett (Ed O'Neill), a successful owner of a closets and blinds company, and his children. What results is a comedic look at different modern American family structures, from nuclear to blended to same-sex.

Played by Sofia Vergara, Gloria is Jay's younger, feisty, fun-loving Colombian second wife. She moved to the US with her son Manny, whom she dotes on, often to the frustration of no-nonsense, tough-love Jay. As much as he adores Gloria, her voice is known for driving the next-door neighbor's dog crazy and setting off car alarms.

The tale of how Gloria got to the States always hangs over her: she stole an opportunity to leave for America from her sister Sonia, and her past in Colombia regularly comes back to haunt her when she least needs it.

Gloria is firmly superstitious. She thinks that her family is cursed because her great-great-grandfather made a deal with the devil, causing many of her relatives to end up in jail.

What better way to celebrate Gloria's Colombian origins than a drink based on the country's favorite traditional liqueur? The standard components of a sour cocktail are here, but rather than whiskey, gin, or amaretto (some of the more popular bases), this one uses the anise-flavored aguardiente, or "guaro," as it's known colloquially. It's a liqueur with only four ingredients—water, sugar, alcohol, and anise—and so its flavor profile is quite simple, allowing it to fit nicely into a classic drink format. It is only recommended if you like anise!

Alcatraz

OZ
LEO GLYNN | ERNIE HUDSON
DRAMA • USA • 1997

1½ shots añejo tequila
¾ shot oloroso sherry
½ shot gentian liqueur
¼ shot mezcal
⅙ shot agave syrup
8 drops chocolate bitters
Garnish: orange zest

Stir all ingredients with ice, strain into an ice-filled Old Fashioned glass, and garnish.

Oz chronicles the daily activities of an unusual prison unit known as "Emerald City" and its male inhabitants. This experimental wing is run by Tim McManus, who is on a mission to rehabilitate the inmates, teaching them responsibility rather than simply punishing them for their crimes.

The prison warden at Oz is Leo Glynn, played by Ernie Hudson. Glynn began working as a corrections officer in the early 1960s, and, as a result, adopts an old-fashioned approach to the way he helps run the place, focusing more on retribution than rehabilitation. Glynn runs the entire prison, while answering mainly to Governor James Devlin–a right-wing politician whom he often clashes with due to policy disagreements.

It is obvious that Glynn is well respected by the staff, and his fair approach with the prisoners is evident. However, he can be petty and vindictive at times, riding the fine line between ethically sound and morally negligent to get the job done.

While *Oz* is set in a fictional maximum-security prison, the most famous real-life penitentiary is surely that which sits on its own island in the San Francisco Bay: Alcatraz. The cocktail carrying its name was found by the late Gaz Regan, a key figure in the modern popularization of mixology and a prolific collector of recipes from around the world. He discovered this recipe by Christin Wagner, who created the drink in 2015 at La Petite Grocery in New Orleans. With its unusual mix of tequila, mezcal, sherry, and chocolate, this beverage is high in alcohol, but makes a great pre-dinner cocktail.

Appletini

SCRUBS
JOHN MICHAEL "J.D." DORIAN | ZACH BRAFF
SITCOM • USA • 2001

This offbeat medical sitcom ran for nine seasons, spanning the 2000s. The show follows J.D. (Zach Braff) and Turk (Donald Faison) as they graduate from medical school and embark on a career at Sacred Heart Hospital. On that same internship is Elliot Reid, J.D.'s on-off girlfriend. Together these fresh-faced junior doctors navigate the comedy and tragedy of life in a hospital, always under the watchful eye of their mentor, Chief of Medicine Dr. Perry Cox.

But life won't be easy if Dr. Cox has anything to do with it. His sergeant-major-like treatment of them is designed to prepare the newbies for the harsh realities of life in a busy hospital. J.D. has a tough time at first, but ultimately finds his feet.

2 shots vodka
1 shot apple schnapps
½ shot Cointreau
½ shot fresh lemon juice
Garnish: cocktail cherry

Shake all ingredients with ice, strain into a chilled Martini glass, and garnish.

The Appletini, J.D.'s go-to order at the bar, is a confection of a drink with apple, citrus, and sweetness all vying for palate space. Its origin is unknown, and probably came about as it was the obvious cocktail to make with any apple schnapps lying around. Recipes vary, but many are too sweet, so these proportions are designed to avoid that.

ARRESTED DEVELOPMENT
GEORGE MICHAEL BLUTH | MICHAEL CERA
SITCOM • USA • 2003

Arrested Development gained nothing short of cult status in its first three seasons of fast-paced, chaotic hilarity with the Bluth family (it has since returned for two further seasons). The style of the show is that of a fly-on-the-wall documentary, with a single handheld camera capturing the family's capers as they happen.

This is a tough family to grow up in. Entrepreneurial pursuits come first, and the kids and grandkids are just pulled along for the ride ... and forced to work for their parents. The young George Michael's job is manning the banana stand, a kiosk on the Oceanside Wharf boardwalk that sells frozen bananas (an original Bluth family innovation) served with a variety of toppings such as hot fudge, chocolate, and nuts.

. . . .

6 shots pineapple juice

2 shots coconut cream

1 shot light (single) cream

1 ripe banana

Garnish: pineapple wedge and cocktail cherry

Blend all ingredients with a cup of crushed ice, pour into a chilled Hurricane glass, and garnish.

A tribute to Bluth's Original Frozen Banana Stand–the last bastion of the family's crumbling business empire–this drink will please anyone with a taste for the tropical.

Essentially a virgin Piña Colada with banana, this is practically a meal in a glass. You can make it into a more grown-up drink with the addition of 2 shots of light rum, but the mocktail version is the tastiest way to enjoy this exotic delight.

FAWLTY TOWERS
BASIL FAWLTY | JOHN CLEESE
SITCOM • UK • 1975

Considered one of the greatest British comedy series of all time, *Fawlty Towers* opens the doors to short-tempered, arrogant, and completely inept hotel owner Basil Fawlty and his no-nonsense wife Sybil as they attempt to run their Torquay inn. Joining Basil and Sybil are their two loyal but long-suffering staff members, Polly the peacekeeping chambermaid and Manuel the incompetent waiter.

Basil, played by Monty Python member John Cleese, is on a never-ending mission to raise the tone of his establishment, constantly contriving new ways to attract a high-end clientele. Yet his snobbish nature and loathsome attitude toward the public often leave him in hot water, and he is repeatedly berated by his wife.

Basil's frustrations and exasperated manner extend beyond the guests, often leading to fractious encounters with his staff. Hard-working but disorganized waiter Manuel struggles to keep up given his rudimentary grasp of English, often leading to hilarious mishaps with hotel patrons and Mr. Fawlty himself, which cool-headed Polly must then defuse.

....

If there's one kitchen store cupboard ingredient that was born to live its best life in cocktails, it is marmalade. This unlikely and overlooked addition is a mixology marvel, bringing bitter orange depth like nothing else, provided you choose the best stuff in the store (or, even tastier, homemade).

Either way, this "breakfast drink" can of course be consumed at any time of the day (7 a.m. cocktails aren't recommended anyway). It's a more mellow and sweet concoction than the classic Martini that will ease less experienced guests into the category. Just be sure to dissolve your marmalade fully so that all of it makes it through the strainer and into the final serve.

2 shots gin

1 heaped bar spoon marmalade

⅓ shot triple sec

⅓ shot fresh lemon juice

Garnish: small triangle of toast

Add the gin and marmalade to a shaker. Stir vigorously until the marmalade has dissolved. Add remaining ingredients and shake with ice. Fine-strain into a chilled Martini glass and garnish.

TWIN PEAKS
DALE COOPER | KYLE MACLACHLAN
MYSTERY DRAMA • USA • 1990

FBI Special Agent Dale Cooper (Kyle MacLachlan) arrives in the sleepy, rural town of Twin Peaks, Washington, to a community rocked by a brutal discovery: a local logger has found the corpse of beautiful, popular homecoming queen Laura Palmer wrapped in a sheet of plastic.

As Agent Cooper begins to carry out his investigation of the murder, he uncovers disturbing evidence that suggests Laura's death was linked to the slaying of another young woman the previous year. He alerts the townspeople that the killer is likely someone from their own area.

Courteous, eccentric, and prone to strangely spiritual dreams, Agent Cooper quickly gains the acceptance and respect of the region's residents. But as shock and fear spread, he uncovers that Laura may not have been as innocent as she seemed, with her demise setting off a chain reaction of events that shake the town to its very core.

One of the most popular shows of the 1990s, and later revived for a limited run in 2017, *Twin Peaks* gained international acclaim due to creator David Lynch's unique brand of surrealism.

Given the cult status of the show, some considerable detective work among fans has gone into picking apart the scene in which this drink is served up. Analysis of the bar's contents and the appearance of the beverage itself suggest this recipe, or something very similar. The key to nailing the distinctive cocktail's look is the blueish foam the coffee base is topped with. If all goes well, you'll have a perky and surreal take on an Irish coffee, the perfect tipple to see you through a *Twin Peaks* viewing marathon.

1 shot bourbon

6 shots freshly brewed coffee

1 shot blue curaçao

1 egg white

Splash of club soda (soda water)

Build (that is, add the ingredients sequentially in-glass as opposed to in a shaker) the drink in an ice-filled Collins glass. First, pour in the bourbon and coffee. Blend the blue curaçao, egg white, and club soda separately until they form a voluminous froth. Use this to add a large white head to the drink, and serve.

Blackberry Gin & Tonic

FLEABAG
FLEABAG | PHOEBE WALLER-BRIDGE
COMEDY DRAMA • UK • 2016

This show gives viewers a hilarious and heart-breaking look at the witty, frustrated mind of Fleabag, a free-spirited thirtysomething trying to make sense of her life in modern-day London. From tackling the grief of losing her best friend, to awkwardly navigating a series of relationships and cringeworthy sexual encounters, Fleabag is a woman working to heal.

The show opens with our main character facing the reality of her current situation. Having failed to secure a loan to keep her small guinea-pig-themed café afloat, and recently split from her partner, Harry, she finds herself looking for intimacy wherever she can find it. Simultaneously, she tries to maintain a relationship with her over-achieving sister, Claire, as well as her widowed father and his new partner, who just so happens to be godmother to both women.

Fleabag breaks the fourth wall, allowing audiences a front-row seat to the character's clever, dark thoughts. Creator and writer Phoebe Waller-Bridge plays the lead role; the show is based on her popular one-woman play of the same name.

Fleabag can be a prickly character at times, so a brambly twist on her favorite drink seems fitting. This is an impressive yet simple way to elevate a standard gin and tonic, both in terms of aesthetic beauty, and with the extra depth of flavor that comes from fresh blackberries (defrosted from frozen is fine too) and a hint of rosemary.

Handful of blackberries

1 shot fresh lemon juice

1½ shots gin

½ shot sugar syrup

3 shots tonic water

Garnish: 1 blackberry

In a shaker, muddle most of the blackberries with lemon juice. Add gin and sugar syrup, and shake with ice. Strain into an ice-filled copa de balon (gin balloon) and top with tonic water. Submerge a few blackberries in the drink, with a sprig or two of rosemary running around the glass to give the illusion of brambles (and that fantastic aroma).

FARGO
LESTER NYGAARD | MARTIN FREEMAN
BLACK COMEDY/CRIME DRAMA • USA • 2014

A black comedy crime drama inspired by the popular 1996 Coen brothers film of the same name, *Fargo* is a gripping saga of survival in a cutthroat world. Each season follows a different story, but the first tells the tale of Lester Nygaard, played by Martin Freeman. He's an ordinary guy who sells insurance in his hometown of Bemidji, Minnesota, and has been treated badly and mocked his whole life. However, everything changes after a chance encounter at the hospital with a man named Lorne Malvo (Billy Bob Thornton). This stranger takes it upon himself to kill Lester's long-time bully, telling Lester he should start standing up to those who harass or belittle him.

From that moment on, the spineless Lester's morals become downright nefarious. He murders, steals from, and frames others, becoming inured to the suffering he causes. As he becomes tangled in a web of misdemeanors, his life becomes about running away from his crimes … until he runs out of road.

¾ **shot** blended Scotch

¾ **shot** sweet vermouth

¾ **shot** cherry liqueur

¾ **shot** orange juice

Garnish: orange zest

Shake all ingredients with ice, fine strain into a chilled Martini glass, and garnish.

This drink first appeared in *The Savoy Cocktail Book*, now a key source text for modern mixologists. The legendary tome was authored in 1930 by the head bartender at London's Savoy Hotel, Harry Craddock. The luxury hotel's American Bar, where he plied his trade and invented several drinks, stands to this day, and is regularly awarded the title of the world's best. The Blood & Sand, ordered by Lester after he wins an "Insurance Salesman of the Year" award in Las Vegas, is made up of an unlikely combination of ingredients, sounding like a sticky-sweet mess–on paper, at least. But, as you sip, the cascade of different flavors work in beautiful harmony.

GAME OF THRONES
DAENERYS TARGARYEN | EMILIA CLARKE
FANTASY DRAMA • USA • 2011

2 shots reposado tequila

3 shots blood orange juice

1 shot fresh lime juice

1 shot sugar syrup or agave syrup

Garnish: blood orange slices; lime and salt for rimming glass

Add all ingredients to a shaker with ice and shake. Strain into a coupe glass and garnish.

Game of Thrones earned its place as one of the most popular television shows in history through a heady blend of sex, violence, and sheer unpredictability. Over the course of eight action-packed seasons, it chronicles the ongoing fight for control of the Seven Kingdoms. But the nine noble families at war with one another have a darker foe from the frozen north to contend with if they are to take the Iron Throne. In this game, you either win or you die.

Daenerys Targaryen (Emilia Clarke), a royal in exile, is one of the last surviving members of her House. The Targaryens once ruled Westeros, but now are just one of many factions fighting to recapture the throne. Sold off to brutal husband Khal Drogo (Jason Momoa), leader of the nomadic Dothraki clan, the experience transforms her from a naive teen to a courageous mother of dragons, ready to fight for her birthright by any means necessary.

Westeros is an unforgiving place, with no one heroic enough to be spared. This blood-red cocktail brings together the fire of reposado tequila with the ice and zesty respite of lime and blood orange. Peel the blood orange slices and mount them on the rim for that extra grisly effect.

1½ shots Irish whiskey

½ shot amaro

½ shot coffee liqueur

½ shot espresso

Garnish: 3 coffee beans

Add all ingredients to a cocktail shaker with ice and shake. Strain into a coupe glass and garnish.

FRIENDS
RACHEL GREEN | JENNIFER ANISTON
SITCOM • USA • 1994

Join the best-known group of friends in sitcom history as they navigate twenty-something life in New York City. The crew includes Rachel (Jennifer Aniston), a pampered fashion enthusiast, Joey (Matt LeBlanc), a wannabe actor and ladies' man, Monica (Courteney Cox), a cleaning-obsessed chef, Chandler (Matthew Perry), a socially awkward but hilarious data analyst, Phoebe (Lisa Kudrow), a hippie masseuse and musician, and Ross (David Schwimmer), a brainy paleontologist who never quite manages to find luck with women.

The show opens as the gang meet at their local coffee shop and favorite hangout spot, Central Perk, when in bursts Rachel, clad in a wedding dress, having run away from her betrothed at the altar. She reconnects with her childhood bestie, Monica, and the group welcomes Rachel with open arms. But the reunion is less than sweet for Ross, who has struggled with his feelings for Rachel since high school. Rachel soon settles in with the group, moving in with Monica and determined to pursue her dream of taking on the fashion world, while the rest of the friends struggle with their own ambitions.

The two best-known coffee-based drinks at any bar are the Espresso Martini and the Irish Coffee. They're both delicious ways to enjoy café culture in a cocktail glass, so which one to choose? Well, with this drink, you can have both.

The amaro adds botanical depth, giving the cocktail a somewhat medicinal edge. This Italian herbal liqueur is traditionally consumed neat after dinner. It's sweet and packed with flavors from the herbs, roots, flowers, bark, and citrus peels that traditionally go into it. Any Italian brand of amaro will work, but they are all different, prepared using recipes that originated in monasteries or pharmacies hundreds of years ago.

Cookie Martini

1½ shots vanilla vodka

1½ shots Irish cream liqueur

1 shot amaretto liqueur

Rim: sugar sprinkles

Shake all ingredients with ice, then strain into a Martini glass rimmed with sugar sprinkles.

EMPIRE
LORETHA "COOKIE" LYON | TARAJI P. HENSON
DRAMA • USA • 2015

Set in New York City, musical drama *Empire* is centered on the fictional hip-hop and showbiz company Empire Entertainment. The show depicts the ins and outs of a constant battle for control of the business among its founding family's members.

Mogul Lucious Lyon (Terrence Howard) is forced to choose a successor among his sons, who are vying for power over his multi-million-dollar enterprise. At the same time, his ex-wife Loretha "Cookie" Lyon (Taraji P. Henson) tries to reclaim what is hers after being released from a 17-year prison sentence.

Before the success of Empire Entertainment, Cookie was a prolific drug dealer who helped Lucious achieve a fruitful career with the money she made illegally. Together, they have three children: business-savvy Andre, who is already Empire's CEO, R&B singer Jamal, and aspiring rapper Hakeem. Cookie puts her kids first, being as ruthless as necessary to ensure that they have access to the best life has to offer.

Cookies aren't the most obvious inspiration for cocktails, but given the growing number of cream, nut, and chocolate liqueurs now available, there are limitless options for recreating everyone's favorite baked treat.

This simple concoction calls for vanilla vodka—one of the easiest infused vodkas to find—blended with Irish cream and amaretto (almond) liqueurs. The result is something akin to freshly baked cookies with a boozy backbone. It's a fine dessert drink, and, decorated with multi-colored sprinkles, it makes quite the entrance after dinner.

THE FRESH PRINCE OF BEL-AIR
WILL SMITH | WILL SMITH
SITCOM • USA • 1990

A quintessential '90s sitcom, *The Fresh Prince of Bel-Air* follows Will Smith (played by Will Smith) as he leaves West Philadelphia–where he was born and raised–to navigate a brand-new, privileged life in California.

After he gets into a fight while playing basketball, Will's mother sends him off to live with their wealthy relatives in Bel-Air, Los Angeles. He moves in with his strict uncle, Philip Banks, and no-nonsense aunt, Vivian, as well as his stuck-up cousins Carlton and Hilary, gullible Ashley, and baby Nicky, who often find themselves the butt of Will's jokes.

The street-smart teenager is also cared for by the family's cynical English butler, Geoffrey, whom Will mistakes for his uncle Philip when he first arrives at their impressive mansion. As Will explores the upper-class world he has found himself in, he frequently gets himself and his family in trouble, often with hilarious consequences. As the show progresses, we see his character grow from an irresponsible teenager into a mature young man.

....

This Hotel Bel-Air Bar & Lounge favorite was created by celebrity chef Wolfgang Puck and continues to impress thanks to its perfectly balanced flavors. The drink is the epitome of refined elegance, in keeping with its birthplace in the star-studded neighborhood. With its multi-layered fruit notes, it is a nicely elevated mocktail that won't have sober guests feeling left out. You can also dress it beautifully using rose petals and a raspberry on the rim to make it a toast-worthy tipple.

8 raspberries

1 shot cranberry juice

1 shot lychee purée

2/3 shot grenadine

½ shot rose water

½ shot sugar syrup

½ shot fresh lemon juice

Garnish: 1 rose petal and 1 raspberry

In a cocktail shaker, muddle raspberries. Add remaining ingredients and shake well with ice. Strain into a red wine glass and garnish.

SEINFELD
JERRY SEINFELD | JERRY SEINFELD
SITCOM • USA • 1989

Seinfeld centers on the misadventures of New York City stand-up comedian Jerry Seinfeld (played by Jerry Seinfeld) and his friends: the equally neurotic George (Jason Alexander), sarcastic publishing world underling Elaine (Julia Louis-Dreyfus), and wacky neighbor Kramer (Michael Richards). Each episode is like a rollercoaster, following Jerry and his pals as they maneuver through everyday life–careers, relationships, and more.

Throughout the show, Jerry is an eternal optimist. He rarely runs into major problems and is the only character to maintain the same career throughout the show. He loves his job, and many of his jokes are based on observations about his love life, awkward personal moments, and his friends' quirky habits. And although he seems to have a new girlfriend every week, his relationships never last.

Widely described as a "show about nothing," *Seinfeld* is seen as one of the most influential sitcoms of all time due to its whip-smart observations of the minutiae that make us human. It set the mold for those who came after it, including co-writer and producer Larry David's alt-comedy hit *Curb Your Enthusiasm*.

In a season 2 episode, as Jerry waits for ex-girlfriend Elaine to join him for dinner, her intimidating father who's visiting the city isn't making the awkward hanging about any less uncomfortable. Drinks are ordered in the interim, and Jerry blurts out, "I'll have a cranberry juice with two limes."

It's curious that, in a show about a stand-up comedian, there is almost no mention of alcohol over the course of 180 episodes. So here, this innocuous drink is spiced up a little. It can be a showstopper if presented in a copper mug, and either way, it can be made into a nice holiday drink for sober guests with the addition of a cinnamon stick.

2 shots cranberry juice

4 shots ginger beer

2 lime wedges

Garnish: lime slice and fresh cranberries

Fill a copper mule mug (or an Old Fashioned glass, if you don't have one) with crushed ice (you can crush your own by bashing cubes wrapped in a dish towel). Add the cranberry juice and ginger beer before squeezing the lime wedges into the drink, and garnish. For a festive touch you can add a cinnamon stick too, which will give it something of a winter spice aroma when sipping.

Dirty Martini

THE MARVELOUS MRS. MAISEL
MIRIAM "MIDGE" MAISEL | RACHEL BROSNAHAN
PERIOD COMEDY/DRAMA • USA • 2017

Miriam "Midge" Maisel seems to have it all: the perfect husband, two kids, and a beautiful apartment on New York's Upper West Side. Like any good 1950s Jewish woman, she is a staunch cheerleader for her husband, Joel, an aspiring stand-up comedian. But her seemingly flawless life takes a sudden turn when Joel leaves Midge for his secretary, and Midge discovers she has an unexpected talent herself.

Played by Rachel Brosnahan, the show's eponymous main character is highly organized, friendly, and outgoing, known for her immaculate taste. Working at department store B. Altman, she has a passion for makeup, but she soon realizes that her true love is performance, specifically stand-up comedy. Not only does she enjoy it, she's good at it too.

This life-changing realization sees Midge embark on a journey through the bars and nightclubs of Greenwich Village as she uses her newfound talent to reinvent her life and pursue a career in comedy, aided by her brusque manager, Susie (Alex Borstein). But will Midge achieve her dream in a male-dominated field?

2 shots gin

½ shot dry vermouth

Splash of olive brine

Garnish: thin lemon twist

Shake all ingredients with ice, fine strain into a chilled Martini glass, and garnish.

Olives with gin is a classic flavor combination that works brilliantly. It's hardly surprising, then, that some curious soul once wondered what it might be like if a little more of that tangy olive juice made its way into the Martini glass. Turns out it's a very tasty drink for anyone who likes olives—which Midge clearly does, as she partakes in this cocktail often throughout the show. But beware: include too much of the brine and the cocktail will be ruined. Even worse, if the substrate your olives came in is in fact oil or some sort of flavored dressing, it will be undrinkable.

Dubonnet Cocktail

1½ shots gin
¾ shot Dubonnet Rouge
Garnish: lemon slice

Stir ingredients with ice, strain into a rocks glass with one or two very large ice cubes, and garnish.

THE CROWN
QUEEN ELIZABETH II | OLIVIA COLMAN
HISTORICAL DRAMA • UK • 2016

Critically acclaimed historical drama *The Crown* takes a look behind the gates of Buckingham Palace at the life of Britain's longest-reigning monarch in history, Queen Elizabeth II.

The show begins in 1947, telling the tale of how the young and newlywed Princess Elizabeth took her place at the head of the royal family following the death of her father, King George IV, in 1952. Chronicling the Queen and other royals through some of the most significant events in modern British history, it covers political turmoil, an empire in decline, and a fractious household dynamic. Shaped by hundreds of years of the strict royal regime, the family tries its best to remain relevant and relatable in a rapidly shifting world.

Throughout all this we're treated to a lavish production with opulent sets and costumes that transport viewers back in time, with the Queen always dressed immaculately in her famously considered outfits (and hats!).

Dubonnet was created in the 1830s to promote the intake of quinine among the French Foreign Legionnaires stationed in North Africa. The idea was that, if quinine was an antimalarial, what better way to encourage the troops to take it regularly than by creating a tasty botanical aperitif containing the substance?

The Dubonnet Cocktail itself has been a favorite of royalty for some time. The Queen Mother was known to be a big fan, and it has been confirmed by various sources to also have been the preferred tipple of her eldest daughter, Queen Elizabeth II. She reportedly took it served in a rocks glass, with the lemon slice beneath the ice.

Elderflower Gin Fizz

2 shots gin

1 shot elderflower liqueur

1 shot fresh lemon juice

Prosecco to top

Garnish: lemon zest

Shake the gin, elderflower liqueur, and lemon juice with ice. Strain into a Champagne flute, top with chilled Prosecco, and garnish.

INSECURE
ISSA DEE | ISSA RAE
COMEDY DRAMA • USA • 2016

Insecure follows the good times, awkward experiences, and racy encounters of non-profit employee Issa Dee (played by the show's creator, Issa Rae) and high-flying lawyer Molly Carter, who have been BFFs since their college days at Stanford. The show captures their triumphs and mishaps alike as they go through life in sunny, hip, multicultural Los Angeles.

In the show, the fashionable duo are forced to deal with their flaws as they attempt to navigate different worlds, both personal and professional, and cope with an endless catalogue of issues. Issa tries to figure out what she wants out of life and how to take control of it, while fumbling through the journey. Meanwhile, her boyfriend, Lawrence, who has fallen victim to complacency, works hard to get his own plan together too.

However, this relationship is perhaps not built to last, and Issa tries to embrace single life—quickly realizing it's not as easy as it sounds. She takes solace in hanging with Molly and the rest of their friend group, including self-styled comedienne Kelli and the pretentious, put-together Tiffany, as well as hooking up with charismatic men in her orbit.

Insecure explores the Black American experience, highlighting all the city of LA has to offer its young inhabitants.

. . . .

Issa's initial go-to drink on *Insecure* is Prosecco with a gin floater (later in the show, the gin is replaced by vodka). Either way, this boozy concoction is a good place to start. In fact, Prosecco, the Italian sparkling wine that's become so popular in recent years, goes particularly well with gin; they appear together in innumerable recipes. Here, elderflower liqueur is added to round off the cocktail with floral notes and sweetness, with lemon juice to keep it balanced and bring out the other flavors in a crisp, summery tipple.

AMERICAN HORROR STORY: COVEN
MARIE LAVEAU | ANGELA BASSETT
HORROR • USA • 2013

Set in New Orleans, *Coven* is the third season of the anthology show *American Horror Story*. As with other seasons, this one boasts a standalone storyline, following descendants of the women who survived the infamous Salem witch trials in seventeenth-century Massachusetts. Some don't even know of their heritage until the reality is forced upon them—in traumatic fashion.

The gals who carry this bloodline all end up at Miss Robichaux's Academy for Exceptional Young Ladies, where they're somewhat sheltered from the outside world and taught how to wield their magical abilities. But, as at any boarding school, life for the students is often laden with plenty of drama—from both power struggles and romantic interests.

The Marie Laveau character is based on a real person: the "Voodoo Queen" of New Orleans. Laveau plied her trade as a professional practitioner of the occult in the mid-nineteenth century. In the show Marie is highly fictionalized, and immortal: we see her life extending well into the twentieth century. She doesn't like witches at all, particularly the witch trial descendants, but a friendship with witch Fiona changes all that as they forge a diabolical alliance.

1½ shots gin
½ shot fresh lemon juice
¼ shot sugar syrup
Champagne to top
Garnish: lemon twist

Shake the gin, lemon juice, and sugar syrup with ice. Strain into a flute, top up slowly with Champagne, and garnish.

Marie shares a celebratory French 75 with ally Fiona after slaying the men of the Delphi Trust. Whether you're toasting the demise of witch hunters or not, this is the perfect cocktail for any special occasion. It consists of Champagne (or Prosecco, which some prefer) armed with the alcoholic oomph of gin and the citrus bite of lemon juice, all rounded off with a little sugar sweetness.

The drink allegedly originated in the battlefields of France during World War I. British soldiers combined what was at hand—London gin from home—with the local Champagne. It was named after the iconic French M1897 75mm artillery gun due to its hard-hitting nature.

DESPERATE HOUSEWIVES
GABRIELLE "GABY" SOLIS | EVA LONGORIA
COMEDY DRAMA • USA • 2004

Welcome to Wisteria Lane, an idyllic, picturesque suburb masking a secret world of gossip, scandal, and, on occasion, murder.

Desperate Housewives follows the lives of a close-knit group of women in the wake of the unexpected, shocking suicide of one of the neighborhood's residents. Gabrielle "Gaby" Solis (Eva Longoria), a former successful runway model-turned-resentful housewife, lives with her wealthy, career-obsessed husband Carlos in the largest lot on the lane. However, their money and social status cannot hide their unhappy marriage, with the show beginning as Gaby finds herself embroiled in a sordid affair with the couple's gardener.

Her troubles only increase as she becomes entwined in the mysterious lives of the other local residents, whose neatly manicured lawns and carefully arranged flowerbeds hide a multitude of troubled lives and deadly family secrets.

What caused the suicide of their seemingly happy neighbor, whose perfect existence had been the cause of much envy? All is not what it seems for the *Desperate Housewives*.

2 shots tequila blanco

½ shot triple sec

1 shot fresh lime juice

1 teaspoon agave nectar

Garnish: lime wedge

Combine all ingredients in a blender with crushed ice, and blend. Or, for the classic non-frozen straight-up serve, shake and strain into either a chilled, salt-rimmed Margarita glass or an ice-filled rocks glass for a longer-lasting drink. Garnish.

The mighty Margarita is, by some measures, the most ordered cocktail in America (and Gaby's go-to drink). It first rose to popularity in 1940s Mexico and America, slowly spreading around the world in the '50s thanks to increasing global travel as well as its inclusion in prominent mixology manuals.

Today, there are countless variations on the Margarita; it could be a considered a whole category of cocktails. At its heart is almost always the interplay between tequila, lime, and bittersweet orange flavors. This version provides a real crowd-pleasing serve, with blended crushed ice. It's a delicious, boozy slushy.

30 ROCK
LIZ LEMON | TINA FEY
SITCOM • USA • 2006

Having become known for her work on *Saturday Night Live*, Tina Fey created *30 Rock* as a parody of what goes on behind the scenes of a topical satirical sketch show. As is typical of fast-paced media operations, the real drama takes place off camera, amid internal politics, ego battles, and romantic entanglements.

Fey plays a version of herself, Liz Lemon, creator and writer of *The Girlie Show*. Socially awkward and a self-confessed geek (particularly when it comes to *Star Wars*), she's constantly pulled in opposing directions. Above her is the network with its commercial demands, always prepared to compromise the show to gain ratings. Below her is a team of writers and stars, often incompetent and sometimes chaotic, needing constant babysitting to keep it together.

2 shots white wine

Sprite to top

Garnish: lemon wedge

Fill a highball glass with ice and pour in the wine. Tilt the glass, slowly pour in Sprite (which can be very fizzy), and garnish.

Sure, it's just a white wine spritzer, right? Well, Liz Lemon's favorite drink, Funky Juice, packs a certain kind of punch. The heavy sweetness of the lemon-limey soda isn't for everyone, but paired with a fruity wine such as a Sauvignon Blanc, a Riesling, or perhaps a Pinot Noir, this is a deliciously drinkable tipple. On *30 Rock* the ice is listed as an ingredient, and its importance can't be overstated. You'll need it to reach all the way above the rim of your glass to make sure you tame the Sprite and keep the drink crisp.

Liz likes to keep a Thermos flask of Funky Juice next to her toilet. It probably does have some handy cleaning properties given the ingredients, but it'd be nicer to make it fresh, garnishing with a thick slice of lemon to bring out the zesty undertones of both the wine and soda.

Gibson

THE QUEEN'S GAMBIT
BETH HARMON | ANYA TAYLOR-JOY
PERIOD DRAMA • USA • 2020

The Queen's Gambit follows chess prodigy Beth Harmon as she develops her game and navigates through the cutthroat world of competitive chess.

Orphaned at just nine years old during the Cold War era, Beth is sent to the Methuen Home, a Christian institution for girls. Here, she meets janitor Mr. Shaibel, who ignites her fascination with the chess board. Although he initially refuses to teach her on account of her being female, Beth convinces him to play just one game. Shaibel is victorious, but the match gives Beth a much better understanding of chess tactics and helps her to improve her technique.

After their initial encounter, the pair's games become regular, and Shaibel eventually recognizes that Beth's talent is something truly special. When Beth reaches her teens, she is adopted. She rapidly rises in the chess world, at the same time undergoing personal struggles (including an increasing addiction to alcohol and tranquillizers). Will she overcome her anger and bad habits to defeat the game's innate misogyny and emerge victorious against the world's most skilled players?

2 shots gin

⅓ shot dry vermouth

Garnish: pearl onion on a cocktail stick and a lemon twist

Stir the ingredients in a stirring or mixing glass with ice, strain into a chilled Martini glass, and garnish.

The Gibson—both Beth and her adoptive mother's tipple of choice in *The Queen's Gambit*—is essentially a very dry Martini served with a pearl onion. It may seem like an insignificant variation on the classic Martini, but how dry you take it has been a talking point in mixology for well over a century. It's not known where this specific recipe originated, but some say that, back in the early twentieth century, the onion garnish was simply used as a way to identify the very dry Martinis in a round of otherwise "wet" ones. Back then the standard gin-to-vermouth ratio ranged from 1:1 to 2:1. In more recent years, the vermouth has been dialed down to such an extent that the modern Martini is barely distinguishable from a Gibson, except for the tang of pearl onions.

1 shot grenadine

8 shots cola

Garnish: cocktail cherry

Build the drink in an ice-filled Collins glass, starting with the grenadine. Carefully pour the cola down the side of the angled glass to preserve the red layer of grenadine at the bottom. Garnish with a bright red cocktail cherry and add a straw.

THE A-TEAM
SERGEANT BOSCO ALBERT "B. A." (BAD ATTITUDE) BARACUS │ MR. T
ACTION–ADVENTURE • USA • 1983

The A-Team is a 1980s action-adventure show that follows a group of ex-US Army Special Forces members who were all tried by court martial and wrongfully convicted of a crime during the Vietnam War. They're sentenced to serve time in a military prison, but successfully escape and flee to Los Angeles, where they use their army knowhow to fight oppression and injustice.

Played by Mr. T, B. A. Baracus is the A-Team's driver and mechanic, and has the ability to make impressive machinery out of just about any combination of ordinary parts. He's also known as the group's muscle, performing incredible feats of strength that prove vital in moments of peril. B. A. has an unwavering dislike for his team member Howling Mad Murdock, often calling him a "crazy fool." But over the seasons the pair often save each other's skins, with B. A. growing to love Murdock despite his zany idiosyncrasies.

B. A. has a deep fear of flying and rarely takes to the skies consciously, usually having to be knocked out or tricked before he'll board an aircraft. Instead, he prefers to drive the team's customized GMC van.

One of the most iconic on-screen vehicles in history, the GMC Vandura's color scheme alone is enough to evoke memories of rushing in from playing outside on Saturdays to catch that week's episode of *The A-Team*. And with B. A. being sober, this would have been a perfect beverage to accompany a viewing of the show.

The mocktail is the epitome of 1980s Americana, with all that red, black, cola, and a cherry on top. Anything you can do to dial up that vibe is good, from stripy or bendy straws to fancy swizzle sticks.

THE GOOD PLACE
TAHANI AL-JAMIL | JAMEELA JAMIL
SITCOM • USA • 2016

This sitcom follows Eleanor Shellstrop (Kristen Bell) as she dies and enters the afterlife. Thanks to an administrative error, she goes to the Good Place instead of the Bad Place, where she really belongs. They've got her name right, but everything else they know about her is incorrect.

Eleanor tries to hide her true identity from Good Place architect Michael (Ted Danson) as she attempts to leave her nasty ways behind and earn her keep in the neighborhood, supported by her appointed soulmate Chidi. Wealthy socialite Tahani Al-Jamil, played by Jameela Jamil, is Eleanor's neighbor in the Good Place and the soulmate of Jason (a fellow fraud, like Eleanor). The British philanthropist and model truly believes she belongs in the Good Place and forms an unlikely friendship with Eleanor.

Along with being overly good (she once raised $60 billion for a non-profit organization), one of Tahani's major flaws is frequent name-dropping. But with the support of Eleanor, Chidi, Jason, and Michael, over time, she learns how to be truly righteous.

This aptly named tropical tipple is firmly in the Tiki family of drinks, having been rediscovered by Jeff "Beachbum" Berry and featured in his compendium of "lost" Tiki drinks, *Intoxica!* It was apparently first created at the Top of Toronto restaurant in the CN Tower in the early 1970s. To this day it remains a Tiki classic, with sometimes banana-esque notes.

2 shots white rum

¼ shot crème de cacao

¼ shot coffee liqueur

3 shots pineapple juice

Garnish: pineapple wedge

Shake all ingredients with ice and strain into a Collins glass filled over the brim with crushed ice. Garnish with a pineapple wedge pressed into the ice.

CHEERS
CARLA TORTELLI | RHEA PERLMAN
SITCOM • USA • 1982

"Sometimes you want to go / Where everybody knows your name": probably the most catchy TV theme song ever, and a sentiment that beautifully sums up the coziness of Boston's most famous bar, Cheers.

Throughout the show of the same name, characters share their experiences with each other, whether they are enjoying a drink at the bar or working there. You can barely step into this place without everyone knowing your life story. The backbone of the establishment is Carla, a straight-talking waitress known for taking no prisoners with her acerbic comebacks and scathing one-liners.

During a season 7 episode, the bar enters the city's seventh annual Bloody Mary contest, where they'll be locking horns with arch-rival Gary of the nearby Olde Towne Tavern. He's the Cheers crew's recurring nemesis who always seems to best them, and makes no secret of how much he enjoys doing so.

After last year's loss to Gary in the coveted competition, Carla resolved to never let it happen again. This time around, in an artful bit of chicanery, she has a fake judging panel pretend to award Gary the crown so he goes home happy, not knowing that the real contest will now take place in his absence. Finally, a win for the underdogs and a triumph to celebrate.

....

2 shots vodka

4 shots tomato juice

½ shot fresh lime juice

1 pinch ground black pepper

1 pinch paprika

3 dashes Worcestershire sauce

3 to 4 dashes hot sauce

Garnish: celery stick, skewered olives, and pickles

This can be made in a pitcher by multiplying the ingredients and stirring with ice. But, for a single serving, stir all ingredients with ice in a mixing glass, strain into an ice-filled Collins glass, and garnish.

This brunch cocktail actually seems good for you. Not only does it include the classic tomato juice and Worcestershire sauce, it also has paprika and hot sauce to spice things up and cleanse the soul. In terms of garnish, any popular brunch food is fair game (after all, everything pairs well with tomatoes). But something tangy works best, like olives and pickles. If you don't eat fish, bear in mind that most Worcestershire sauce contains anchovies–although many supermarkets stock similar sauces that are vegetarian.

KNIGHT RIDER
MICHAEL KNIGHT | DAVID HASSELHOFF
ACTION/CRIME DRAMA • USA • 1982

Knight Rider was compulsory viewing for many people in the early 1980s, with kids desperately wishing they had a talking car like K.I.T.T. (Knight Industries Two Thousand). This enigmatic black automobile had its own AI personality and a dashboard console capable of things that seemed pure science fiction in 1982, but have become commonplace today. These features included video calling, TV and music streaming, video games, access to the police database, and more. Today's car owners are still waiting for some of K.I.T.T.'s more situation-specific functionality, however, such as flame throwers, flare launchers, weaponized lasers, and even a built-in cash dispenser.

The show's premise starts with self-made eccentric billionaire Wilton Knight, who rescues undercover LAPD cop Michael Arthur Long (played by David Hasselhoff) after he suffers a near-fatal bullet to the face.

Although everyone thinks that he is dead following the shooting, Michael accepts an offer to have his name changed and his face reconstructed by Knight, creator of Knight Industries and founder of FLAG (Foundation for Law and Government). Knight gives the detective a new identity: Michael Knight. In return, Michael is tasked with becoming a high-tech vigilante, dealing with criminals who operate above the law.

This black-and-red cocktail will evoke memories of television's coolest automobile with a deep, dark ombre effect thanks to the berries, grading from almost black up to an icy-red peak. It's based on a popular variation of the Caipirinha, a Brazilian classic, where the cachaça is substituted with vodka. The addition of berries gives it some extra fruitiness, especially with fresh in-season fruit.

10 fresh blueberries

6 fresh blackberries

2 shots vodka

¾ **shot** sugar syrup

½ **shot** fresh lime juice

Muddle berries in the bottom of an Old Fashioned glass. Add remaining ingredients, fill your glass with crushed ice, and stir. Serve with straws.

MACGYVER
ANGUS "MAC" MACGYVER | RICHARD DEAN ANDERSON
ACTION–ADVENTURE • USA • 1985

Played by Richard Dean Anderson in the original 1985 show, MacGyver is depicted as a genius who speaks multiple languages and has superb engineering skills, an excellent knowledge of applied physics, and military training in bomb-disposal techniques. Oh—and he always has a Swiss Army knife, refusing to carry a gun.

With lots of layers to his character, this non-violent problem solver works for the fictional Phoenix Foundation in Los Angeles as an undercover government agent, where he puts his defense skills to use. Relying on his unconventional expertise to save lives, MacGyver prefers to fight crime with ingenious feats of engineering rather than lethal force. He has an uncanny ability to use any objects in his environment to his advantage. To this day, people widely use the word "MacGyver" as a verb to mean "improvise in a crude-yet-effective way."

⅛ tsp matcha powder

1½ tbsp brown sugar

½ lime, cut into wedges

10 mint leaves

4 shots club soda (soda water)

Garnish: lime slice and mint sprig

Make matcha tea by whisking the powder with 2 shots of hot water. Then, muddle sugar, lime wedges, and mint leaves in a cocktail shaker. Add the matcha tea and shake with ice. Strain into an Old Fashioned glass filled with crushed ice, top with club soda, and garnish.

In the show, MacGyver's father, James, creates a potent cocktail of stimulants and nootropics (no one knows the exact recipe) to enhance soldiers' physical and mental performance. It's a potential game-changer for the Phoenix Foundation, but KX7 doesn't sound like something you'd want to serve to guests: it's untested, and research suggests it could be deadly. This method instead opts for something safe and tasty: a matcha-based Mojito mocktail guaranteed to fire up the senses, mind, and body.

Manhattan

THE HANDMAID'S TALE
OFFRED (JUNE OSBORNE) | ELISABETH MOSS
DRAMA • USA • 2017

An uncomfortable look into a horrifying future, *The Handmaid's Tale* throws viewers into a world of violence, oppression, and religious extremism at unfathomable levels.

Based on the bestselling novel by Margaret Atwood, the show considers a scenario where reproductive rates across the globe have dipped to terrifyingly low numbers and extreme religious groups have taken control. *The Handmaid's Tale* begins in Gilead, a haunting dystopia that once called itself America. It is here that we meet Offred, a handmaid—one of a select few women who remain fertile—who is forcibly ripped from her husband and daughter, stripped of all rights, and enslaved into bearing children for wealthy commanders and their families.

Offred, played by Elisabeth Moss, is placed with a new family after being unable to conceive with her previous commander. Known as June before her capture, she has never allowed her oppression to fully dampen her spirit, plotting to reclaim her stolen daughter and her freedom. But for her and the other handmaids, life is brutal, with flashbacks divulging the alarming reality of how Gilead came to be. Will June find the will to escape? Or will she be forced to live her life as a handmaid, bearing children to whom she holds no claim?

....

2 shots bourbon or rye

1 shot sweet vermouth

2 dashes Angostura bitters

1 dash orange bitters

Garnish: Maraschino or brandied cherry

Stir ingredients in a mixing glass with ice. Strain into a chilled Martini glass and garnish.

Offred gets a rare taste of freedom one night at Jezebel's, a speakeasy-style brothel, and orders a Manhattan—a classic cocktail that every home mixologist should master. It can be made with rye or bourbon whiskey, and with either dry (white) or sweet (red) vermouth.

So, which is the "right" way? It's really down to individual taste, but sweet vermouth is by far the most common option these days. In terms of whiskey, any type will do nicely. The key with such a simple drink is to use quality ingredients. Premium vermouths tend to be a little spicier, and higher-end whiskies are, in general, less sweet.

MIAMI VICE
RICARDO "RICO" TUBBS | PHILIP MICHAEL THOMAS
CRIME DRAMA • USA • 1984

Gripping crime drama *Miami Vice* follows undercover detectives James "Sonny" Crockett (Don Johnson) and Ricardo "Rico" Tubbs (Philip Michael Thomas), along with their extended team, through the mean streets of Miami, Florida.

Rico is an ex-NYPD police officer who travels to the city to seek revenge on the drug lord who killed his fellow cop and brother, Rafael. During this time he meets and joins forces with Sonny, who is coincidentally after the same guy. After catching the criminal, Rico decides to stay on in Miami. This leads to a partnership at the local police department, as the guys collectively take on the city's illegal drug trade and prostitution.

The show majorly influenced men's fashion in the 1980s, popularizing Italian casual, and interior decor that took its inspiration from the Miami look. It also became famous for its cameo guest appearances, which included big-name musicians and actors such as Julia Roberts, Phil Collins, Miles Davis, Gloria Estefan, Wesley Snipes, Little Richard, Bruce Willis, and Leonard Cohen.

2 shots light rum

1 cup chopped strawberries

1 shot fresh lime juice

½ shot sugar syrup

2 shots cream of coconut

2 shots pineapple juice

Garnish: pineapple slice

First, make a Strawberry Daiquiri by blending 1 shot of the rum with strawberries, lime juice, sugar syrup, and 1 cup of crushed ice. Set aside in the freezer. Rinse the blender before adding the remaining shot of rum, cream of coconut, pineapple juice, and 1 cup of crushed ice. Blend until smooth. Layer each blend in a chilled Hurricane glass and garnish.

This is a cocktail like no other in this book, in that it is in fact two classic cocktails layered on top of each other. The combo of a Strawberry Daiquiri and a Piña Colada works fantastically and is a real crowd-pleaser, both visually and gustatorily. Surprisingly, the drink apparently precedes the TV show of the same name, having been spotted in clubs and at beach resorts before *Miami Vice* had ever aired. You can layer the drink in whichever order you like, and if you're really careful you can sit the two halves side-by-side by gently layering them, spoon-by-spoon, up each side of your glass.

MAD MEN
DON DRAPER | JON HAMM
PERIOD DRAMA • USA • 2007

Mad Men provides a window into the heady halcyon days of advertising in New York City in the 1960s. The plot centers around one of Madison Avenue's most prestigious ad agencies, Sterling Cooper, where Don Draper (played by Jon Hamm) serves as creative director. He's the type of guy that can come up with an emotive, evocative campaign idea for any brand, be it air travel or insurance, and then sell it to a wowed client in the boardroom.

Yet, despite being an innovative genius, Don is mercurial at best (some would say downright unreliable). He's got a lot going on under that quiet exterior, thanks to a troubled childhood, traumatic memories of his Korean War duty, and insecurities about his life.

During the show, Don struggles to stay at the top of his game as his past comes back to haunt him, threatening to topple his advertising empire.

This cocktail is as antiquated as its name suggests. It appears in the earliest well-known mixology guide, Jerry Thomas's *How to Mix Drinks*, from 1862. Nothing much has changed since then, although the mid-century *Mad Men*-era of advertising did see a brief rocky patch for this fine drink. In a time dominated by Tiki-style cocktails, the Old Fashioned started to be served with various pieces of fruit and topped with soda, neither of which are welcome here.

Mad Men singlehandedly revived interest in the Old Fashioned in the late noughties, and it remains a staple on bar menus the world over.

2 shots bourbon

½ shot sugar syrup

2 dashes Angostura bitters

Garnish: orange zest

Fill an Old Fashioned glass with ice, pour in ingredients, and stir for at least one minute to allow the mix to cool and dilute properly. If the ice has reduced down slightly, top the glass up with ice. Peel some zest off an orange and fold lengthways over the glass to express the oils. Twist and drop in the glass to garnish.

THE OFFICE (US)
MICHAEL SCOTT | STEVE CARELL
SITCOM • USA • 2005

Have you ever had a boss you love to hate? If so, you might recognize some of the personality traits of Michael Scott, Regional Manager of the Scranton, Pennsylvania, branch of fictional paper company Dunder Mifflin. Completely oblivious and totally ridiculous, Michael (played by Steve Carell) believes in an unconventional managerial approach, armed with a plethora of offensive jokes and outlandish shenanigans, much to the dismay of his colleagues.

The Office (US), based on the UK series of the same name created by Ricky Gervais and Stephen Merchant, gives a hilarious fly-on-the-wall look at the day-to-day life of the Dunder Mifflin employees. The show opens as a documentary-style film crew arrives on the scene to observe modern office life, greeted by an over-enthusiastic Michael and his less-than-thrilled staff, including level-headed receptionist Pam (Jenna Fisher), likeable salesman-cum-prank-lover Jim (John Krasinski), and socially inept Dwight (Rainn Wilson), who is obsessed with impressing Michael.

Despite painting a jolly picture of life at the office, behind closed doors Michael is always anxious about visits from head office, potential restructures, and threats to his branch's future. But somehow he hangs in there, treating viewers to some of television's most awkward comedic moments.

½ **shot** light rum

½ **shot** gin

½ **shot** vodka

½ **shot** tequila blanco

½ **shot** bourbon whiskey

½ **shot** triple sec

½ **shot** sweet vermouth

½ **shot** sugar syrup

½ **shot** fresh lemon juice

½ **shot** fresh lime juice

2 **shots** cola

Garnish: lemon slice; sugar and a lemon wedge to rim

Rim a Collins glass by liberally moistening the rim with a lemon wedge before dabbing it into a saucer of sugar. Shake all ingredients except the cola with ice and strain into your ice-filled glass. Top with cola, and submerge a lemon slice in the drink to garnish.

Of all the cocktails concocted in a fictional TV show, this may be one of the least drinkable—so here, Michael's exact recipe, which appears in a season 3 episode, has been tweaked. He explains that it contains equal parts Scotch, absinthe, rum, gin, vermouth, and triple sec, and two packs of Splenda artificial sweetener. It's (sort of) like a Long Island Iced Tea, but with the added spice of vermouth, absinthe, and whisky, which it turns out can be delicious—*in the right proportions*. Here, the Splenda has been dropped, with a lemon-sugar rim to give a much more suitable, bittersweet finish.

ORANGE IS THE NEW BLACK
SOPHIA BURSET | LAVERNE COX
COMEDY DRAMA • USA • 2013

Orange is the New Black takes place in a women's prison and revolves around the true-life story of Piper Chapman (played by Taylor Schilling), whose history of being romantically entangled with a drug dealer eventually causes her to be sentenced to 15 months in an upstate New York detention center.

Among the large, diverse ensemble cast, one character who defines this comedy drama is Sophia Burset, played by Laverne Cox. Sophia is a transgender inmate at Litchfield Penitentiary who was sentenced after stealing credit cards in order to fund the medical bills for her life-changing transition. She is also one of the prison's hairdressers, running her own salon. Here, Sophia is always happy to lend an ear to fellow inmates, chatting with them about their problems and providing comforting words of wisdom while giving them makeovers.

As the only transgender woman in the prison, Sophia battles with transphobia throughout, while trying everything she can to keep her hormone medication supplied to her.

1 shot Aperol

3 shots orange juice

2 shots peach vodka

Tonic water to top

1 shot black vodka

Slowly build the drink in an ice-filled Collins glass. Pour the ingredients gently over the back of a bar spoon to prevent them mixing, starting with the heaviest. The correct order is Aperol, orange juice, peach vodka, tonic water, and finally a black vodka float.

This drink is the only one in this book to employ black vodka, something you may not have seen but which is widely available, especially online. It's mostly used for building cocktails due to its fairly unique ability to turn drinks black (it often sells out near Halloween).

While some black spirits (such as black tequila) are charcoal-infused, black vodka is usually given its deep color through infusions of wild berries, licorice, or the bark of the acacia tree. The flavor varies, and in most versions it is still very much like regular vodka, but with slight botanical undertones.

24

JACK BAUER | KIEFER SUTHERLAND

ACTION DRAMA • USA • 2001

Based on a truly unique premise, each season of *24* depicts a full day in real time over the course of 24 episodes. One hour at a time, every instalment is packed with intrigue, twists, and cliffhangers as counter-terrorism agent Jack Bauer (played by Kiefer Sutherland) tackles everything from terror plots and assassination attempts to cyber-crime and biological warfare.

Throughout the show Jack ruthlessly pursues his aims, and although that often involves morally questionable tactics or personal loss in the short term, ultimately he's the only character who can be fully trusted. He's not cold and clinical, but emotional–just like the rest of us. He's a father and husband, with plenty of his own personal issues going on in the background. His marriage is rocky at best, and now, his rebellious daughter has gone missing …

1½ shots bourbon

½ shot fresh lime juice

3 dashes Angostura bitters

Ginger beer to top

Garnish: lime wheel

Build in a highball glass over ice and garnish.

This really is the Jack Bauer of cocktails: dependable and ruthlessly direct. But it has soul, and surprising depth. It's a nice way to elevate a mundane Whiskey & Ginger (a fine drink in itself), with the lime keeping the bourbon from over-sweetening things. It's important to serve it ice-cold, in a glass that's full to the brim with cubes, as the sweetness can become too cloying otherwise.

Peach & ginger smash

ATLANTA
EARNEST "EARN" MARKS | DONALD GLOVER
COMEDY DRAMA • USA • 2016

Earnest "Earn" Marks (played by *Atlanta*'s creator Donald Glover) drops out of Princeton, and with no money or prospects he's stuck between staying with his parents and his ex-girlfriend Van (Zazie Beetz). He sees his cousin Alfred gaining minor local success as a rapper under the stage name Paper Boi. With nothing to lose, he persuades Paper Boi that he needs a real manager if he's going to get anywhere in the music industry. This could be a way to win back his ex and improve the future of their daughter, Lottie. With a cunning plan to get his cousin played on local radio, Earn wins the respect of Alfred and gets the job.

Over the seasons the pair go on a bumpy journey toward success, but nothing's ever easy. Poverty could always be around the next corner, and while the show has a humorous take on the matter, the viewer is left feeling uneasy about the state of racial equality in modern America.

1/3 peach, in thin slices

1 thin lemon slice

2 shots bourbon

Ginger ale to top

Garnish: peach slices and mint sprig

In an Old Fashioned glass, muddle three peach slices and the lemon slice to a mushy pulp. Stir in the bourbon, fill the glass with crushed ice, and top with ginger ale. Gently stir and garnish with the remaining peach slices, along with a sprig of mint.

The smash is one of the oldest kinds of cocktail, and is comprised of muddled herbs or fruit along with alcohol and sugar. It originated in the US during the early-to-mid-nineteenth century in the form of the Mint Julep, which contains mint, bourbon, sugar, and water. Over time different spirits have been used, and in more recent years, the smash has opened up to include all kinds of fruits and botanicals. The Julep will always be linked with the South, in particular Kentucky, where it is the official drink of that state's famous Derby event. Here, the smash has been given a distinctively Georgian twist, with fresh peaches and added ginger ale for sweetness and mild spiciness.

Penicillin

ER
DOUG ROSS | GEORGE CLOONEY
MEDICAL DRAMA • USA • 1994

2 shots blended Scotch

¾ shot fresh lemon juice

¾ shot honey-ginger syrup

¼ shot Islay single-malt Scotch

Garnish: candied ginger

Add the blended Scotch, lemon juice, and syrup to a shaker with ice, and shake until well chilled. Strain into a rocks glass filled with ice. Top with the Islay single-malt Scotch and garnish.

At its peak, medical drama *ER* was one of America's top TV shows, running for 15 seasons from the mid-1990s through 2009. Centering around the emergency-room doctors, nurses, and staff of County General Hospital, a fictional level-one trauma center in Chicago, its storylines focus on its employees having to make life-and-death decisions daily.

One of the most popular characters is Dr. Doug Ross, played by George Clooney. He is a passionate physician who continually puts the welfare of his patients, especially children, above his medical career. In fact, during the first season he rescues a boy from a storm drain. The child is flown into County General using a news helicopter, and revived by the pediatrician there.

When he is not saving lives, Ross makes no secret of his love of the opposite sex, going on lots of dates. But after a one-night stand with a woman he picks up in a bar ends in tragedy, he's forced to rethink his ways.

Despite sounding like a prescription, this medicine tastes incredible, and might genuinely soothe your ills in the depths of a sniffly January evening. The cocktail Penicillin was invented in the 2000s by Sam Ross, bartender at Milk & Honey in New York, and has become a staple on bar menus the world over.

It requires the use of honey-ginger syrup, which you'll need to make yourself. To do so, peel and thinly slice 3½ oz (100 grams) of fresh ginger root and combine in a pan with 1 cup (250 ml) honey and 1 cup (250 ml) water. Bring to a boil, reduce the heat, and simmer for 5 minutes. Steep in the fridge overnight and strain through a cheesecloth.

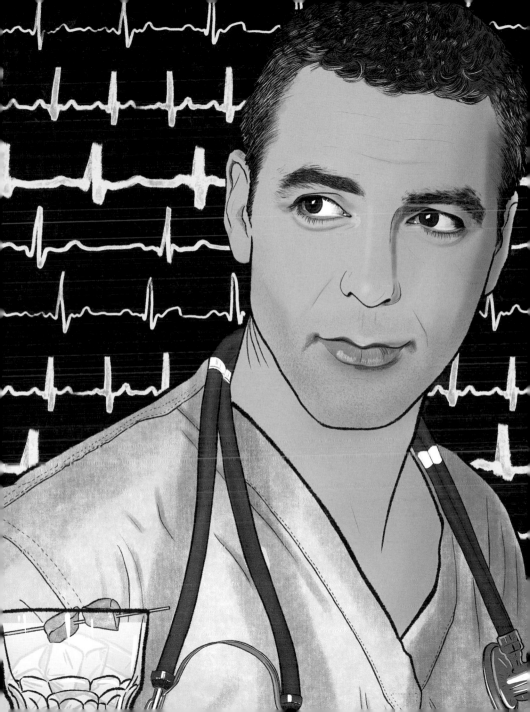

DEUTSCHLAND 83
LENORA RAUCH | MARIA SCHRADER
SPY DRAMA • GERMANY • 2015

Deutschland 83 follows Martin Rauch, a 24-year-old East German native, whose life is upended when he is sent to the West as an undercover spy for the Stasi foreign intelligence service. His mission is to gather as many secrets as possible about NATO's military strategy.

Lenora Rauch, played by Maria Schrader, is Martin's aunt and the cultural attaché at the East German embassy in Bonn. Part of her job is inserting and managing the East's "assets," i.e. spies, in the West. It is Lenora who convinces colleague Walter Schweppenstette to recruit Martin to infiltrate the West German Army. However, after returning to West Germany, she is arrested and questioned about her involvement in the plot.

Martin continues on his mission as tensions between East and West escalate, bringing the threat of nuclear war ever closer. Will he successfully help the world avoid the worst-case scenario?

1 shot peppermint liqueur

1 shot triple sec

2 shots club soda (soda water)

¾ shot fresh lemon juice

Garnish: fresh peppermint sprig

Shake all ingredients except club soda with ice, strain into a chilled Collins glass, top with club soda, and garnish.

In pre-reunification East Germany, consumption of alcohol was high, much more so than in its Soviet Bloc neighbors. Drinks of choice included korn (a grain-based spirit akin to a weaker, unfiltered vodka) and the most popular options, beer and schnapps.

Of all the schnapps-style liqueurs of this period, the peppermint-flavored one made by Pfeffi stands out, and still enjoys an ardent following to this day. This cocktail recipe was created by the brand itself and fuses the unlikely combination of mint and orange into a refreshing, tall sparkler that will beat the heat on even the most searing summer afternoon.

HIGH FIDELITY
ROBYN "ROB" BROOKS | ZOË KRAVITZ
ROMANTIC COMEDY • USA • 2020

Based on the 1995 British novel of the same name by Nick Hornby, *High Fidelity* follows the life of Robyn "Rob" Brooks (played by Zoë Kravitz), a young Brooklynite who owns a record shop called Championship Vinyl.

The show's storylines focus on Rob reliving her past romantic relationships to try and learn what went wrong and why. At the start of the first season she's still reeling from her latest breakup with ex-fiancé Mac, who has left her to move home to London.

Music is a consistent theme in the show, as Rob counts off her top five heartbreaks to a killer soundtrack. Her most mentioned artists are legends such as David Bowie, Prince, and Fleetwood Mac.

Will Rob find her former loves, reconnect with them, and learn something? Or will she needlessly obsess herself into an emotional malaise?

1²⁄₃ shots gin

1 shot fresh lime juice

¾ shot pink grapefruit syrup

²⁄₃ shot egg white

4 drops lavender bitters

Shake all ingredients with ice and strain back into the shaker. Dry shake (without ice) and fine strain into a chilled coupe glass.

High Fidelity is littered with music from across the decades, often heard at pivotal or emotional moments. When Rob catches up with Mac after he breaks her heart, Nick Drake's "Pink Moon" plays, and it's clear there's still something between the pair.

This drink originated in Rome at cocktail bar Must! Creator Marco Michelini says he was inspired by lavender and the ancient traditions surrounding this healthful herb.

Pride Rainbow Slushies

POSE

BLANCA EVANGELISTA | MICHAELA JAÉ RODRIGUEZ

DRAMA • USA • 2018

Makes 6

6 ice pops in different colors

9 shots aged (or spiced) rum

Garnish: skewered cocktail cherries

Unwrap the completely frozen pops and put each color into a different bowl. Divide your rum evenly between the bowls (1½ shots in each). Now mash each ice pop to mix with rum using a fork, before placing the bowls back in the freezer. Next, build each drink in an Old Fashioned glass in the order of the colors of the rainbow, working backward from purple, finishing with red at the top. Garnish each with a cherry and serve right away, or put back in the freezer for serving later, leaving for no longer than two hours.

Set in the 1980s and '90s, *Pose* is a fictional drama that follows members of New York City's Ballroom scene. Popularized by the 1990 documentary film *Paris is Burning*, this real-life subculture was invented as a way for queer people of color to funnel their creativity into pageant-like competitions, dancing and voguing their way to trophies in categories like "femme queen," "first time in drag at a ball," and "realness." Many participants in the scene are part of "houses," made up of chosen family members who provide support systems for each other.

Pose broke ground when actor Michaela Jaé Rodriguez became the first transgender person ever to be nominated for Outstanding Lead Actress in a Drama Series at the 2021 Emmys. On the show she plays Blanca Evangelista, whom we first meet in 1987 when she's a 26-year-old living in the House of Abundance. Often ridiculed for not being as fashionable as other members of her crowd, she's not afraid to stand up for what she believes in.

After being diagnosed with HIV, Blanca decides to take her fate into her own hands and form the House of Evangelista with members of her Ballroom community. As house mother she recruits Damon, Angel (Indya Moore), and Lil Papi, attempting to help guide these young, wayward souls through hard times. Blanca consistently sets the bar for what a parental figure and friend should be, pushing her children to seek new career opportunities beyond sex work.

. . . .

A colorful and tasty way to celebrate Pride Month, these layered slushies will impress guests. Since the festivities occur during summertime, this is a perfect cooldown tipple to beat the heat. You can use any readily available freezer pops, which tend to come in six- or eight-flavor assortment packs—as long as you get most of the rainbow colors covered, you're all set. As each different flavor gets slurped, its unique pairing with the rum will keep things exciting.

BLACK-ISH
RAINBOW JOHNSON | TRACEE ELLIS ROSS
SITCOM • USA • 2014

Award-winning sitcom *black-ish* ran for eight seasons up until 2022, spawning spin-off shows *grown-ish* and *mixed-ish*. The plot is centered around a Black upper-middle-class family led by successful ad executive Andre "Dre" Johnson (Anthony Anderson) and his wife Rainbow (Tracee Ellis Ross), an anesthesiologist. It chronicles their daily lives in a predominately white neighborhood while attempting to maintain a sense of their cultural identity.

Rainbow is at the heart of the show, and is ultimately the only person able to confidently put Dre, who always has crazy ideas, in his place. However, she also has her flaws, such as immense vanity and an obsession with molding her kids to be just like her. Although she may seem assertive on the outside, she has low self-esteem and craves attention, which seems to stem from her lack of praise from her father as a child.

1 shot pineapple juice

1 splash grenadine

¼ shot blue curaçao

½ shot white rum

Pour the pineapple juice into a shot glass and add the grenadine, which should settle at the bottom. Separately, mix the blue curaçao with the vodka and gently float that atop the pineapple shot with a bar spoon.

Celebrate Rainbow by bringing a colorful drink to the party with this Rainbow Shooter. With rum, pineapple, and blue curaçao, it has something of a tropical flavor, and is more pleasant than the average shot (not a cocktail category known for its refined taste profile!).

If you find it all a bit too intense on the palate, you can replace the rum with vodka for a cleaner taste with a tad more fire from the alcohol on the way down. Either way, it's a fun drink that makes a visual impact.

UGLY BETTY

BETTY SUAREZ | AMERICA FERRERA

COMEDY DRAMA • USA • 2006

Young, smart, and stepping headfirst into a world where looks are everything, it'll take all that Betty Suarez has to make it in the cutthroat fashion industry in *Ugly Betty*.

This American comedy drama, based on Colombian telenovela *Yo soy Betty, la fea*, focuses on a Mexican American wannabe writer and fashion disaster with a self-proclaimed "unique" sense of style. Betty, played by America Ferrera, ends up landing a dream job at prestigious New York City fashion magazine *Mode*, where she is hired to quell the scandalous liaisons of publishing mogul Bradford Meade's son Daniel, *Mode*'s newly appointed, womanizing editor-in-chief. The show begins as Betty gets to grips with her new gig in a ruthless industry, surrounded by bright lights, beautiful runway models, and chic designers.

Unhappy with having an assistant as unglamorous as Betty, with her adult braces and odd sartorial choices, Daniel plots to make her quit, giving her a seemingly endless list of embarrassing and unpleasant tasks. But Betty is more resilient than anyone at the magazine could have imagined, and she quickly carves a path for herself there, gaining loyal friends in sharp, Scottish seamstress Christina and nerdy accountant Henry.

Will Betty manage to stay afloat and maintain her sense of self as she juggles a turbulent family life in Queens with the demands of high fashion in Manhattan?

....

The 21 Club in the heart of Manhattan was one of New York Fashion Week's key hangouts, with pretty much every star of fashion and film having walked through its doors over the course of almost 100 years. This landmark venue closed in 2020, but left behind a number of cocktail creations that were invented at the bar there. One such concoction is the aptly named Red Carpet–something special to roll out for guests. It contains some potentially expensive ingredients such as Riesling, Prosecco, and port, and tastes like a genuine slice of the high life.

1 shot Aperol

1 shot tawny port

1 shot gin

1 shot Riesling white wine

1 shot fresh lemon juice

1 shot Prosecco

Garnish: lemon zest

Stir all ingredients except Prosecco with ice in a mixing glass. Fine strain into a Champagne flute, top with Prosecco, and garnish.

Rude Cosmopolitan

SEX AND THE CITY
SAMANTHA JONES | KIM CATTRALL
COMEDY DRAMA • USA • 1998

Kim Cattrall plays the PR-savvy, sensual Samantha Jones in *Sex and the City*, which quickly became a cultural phenomenon after it premiered in 1998. Think fashion, friendship, and plenty of sex!

Over the course of six seasons and two movies, Cattrall brought a healthy dose of glamour, comedy, and relatability to a truly memorable role. Everybody who watched the show wanted to be Samantha. With her own company, runway-ready wardrobe, trendy apartment, and movie-star boyfriend, she's a high-flying woman living the good life in New York.

Portrayed as the most promiscuous of the show's central female foursome, the vast majority of Samantha's storylines revolve around her frequent sexual encounters. However, it's her loyalty to her friends Carrie (Sarah Jessica Parker), Miranda (Cynthia Nixon), and Charlotte (Kristin Davis) that makes her even more lovable. For example, when Carrie confesses that she's having an affair with her married ex-boyfriend Mr. Big (and thus cheating on her current boyfriend, Aidan), Samantha doesn't judge, offering her support instead.

1 shot reposado tequila

1 shot triple sec

1½ shots cranberry juice

½ shot fresh lime juice

2 dashes orange bitters

Shake all ingredients with ice, then fine strain into a chilled Martini glass.

This twist on a regular, vodka-based Cosmo is indeed a cheeky little number. Expect more flavor and depth thanks to the reposado (rested, or slightly aged) tequila. It certainly has that bit of extra bite you'd expect from *SATC*'s sassiest lady. The change in base spirit can have the effect of making an already sweet drink seem very slightly sweeter, so if that's not your thing, add a little extra lime juice to balance it to your liking.

BETTER CALL SAUL
JIMMY MCGILL/SAUL GOODMAN | BOB ODENKIRK
CRIME DRAMA • USA • 2015

This *Breaking Bad* spin-off prequel show sees lawyer Jimmy McGill, or Saul Goodman, as he later becomes known, in the years leading up to his work defending people in the illegal drug trade. From the mail room at his brother's law firm, Jimmy, played by Bob Odenkirk, works hard to get his degree through distance learning at the University of American Samoa. He starts out as a good, honest lawyer fighting for justice, but slowly becomes embroiled with the criminal underworld. After his license is suspended due to fraud, he finally regains it–but under his new flamboyant identity as "Saul Goodman" (inspired by the phrase "it's all good, man"), the go-to guy for some of New Mexico's worst criminals when they're in a pickle.

The story opens in season 1 with Jimmy, or Gene as he's now known, working as a manager in bakery chain Cinnabon. Time has clearly passed after his involvement with *Breaking Bad*'s Walter White (Bryan Cranston) and Jesse Pinkman (Aaron Paul), and this is quite a jump from Jimmy's murky past as a strip-mall lawyer helping drug dealers stay out of jail. After his shift ends, he heads home to a drab, empty apartment where he pours himself a generously sized Rusty Nail, employing an unconventional serve.

2 shots Scotch whisky

⅔ shot Drambuie liqueur

Garnish: orange zest

Pour ingredients into an ice-filled Old Fashioned glass. Stir well to ensure the heavier liqueur is fully mixed and some dilution has occurred. Garnish with a wide strip of orange zest.

To make his cocktail, Jimmy uses equal parts of Drambuie and Dewar's White Label Scotch whisky, which would be far too sweet for most palates. Indeed, even the standard 2 to 1 serve can be a little sweet, and thus a 3 to 1 ratio is recommended here instead. Also, he appears to give it a heavy squirt of store-bought concentrated lemon juice, which for many would render it undrinkable. Instead, serve it with orange zest for a spicy citrus fragrance.

Essentially, a Rusty Nail could be called a "Lazy Old Fashioned." The Drambuie is merely there to temper the fire of Scotch with its sugar and botanicals. But don't let its simplicity deter you. Made with various whiskies (try Laphroaig or Ardbeg for a peaty, smoky take), this is a fine drink for cozy nights in watching TV.

SHERLOCK
SHERLOCK HOLMES | BENEDICT CUMBERBATCH
CRIME DRAMA • UK • 2010

Based on the classic books by Arthur Conan Doyle, this show provides a modernized take on the famous detective and his partner in crime, Dr. John Watson (Martin Freeman). While the key details from Doyle's iconic stories remain the same, Sherlock, played by Benedict Cumberbatch, now lives in twenty-first-century London, working as a consulting detective for Scotland Yard, while Watson is a young veteran of the Afghan war. The pair meet when the eccentric Holmes advertises for a flatmate. Watson responds to the ad and moves into the flat on Baker Street, and it's not long before the pair are solving mysteries and crimes, while constantly working to defeat Sherlock's arch-nemesis, Moriarty (Andrew Scott).

Sherlock is portrayed as a charismatic, high-functioning sociopath with a distinct lack of social graces, who is kept in check by his friend and colleague Dr. Watson. As the world's only consulting detective, he solves crimes through his sheer intellect and is often called upon to handle the most baffling of cases. Together, the pair solve an array of crimes and battle the villains that stand in their path.

The origin of the highball is unclear, though one of mixology's early stars, Patrick Gavin Duffy, claimed to have brought it to America in 1894 after being asked by many Brits to make Scotch and sodas. Duffy ran and worked at several New York bars, and is best known for his post-Prohibition book *The Official Mixer's Manual*, now a classic text.

While a "highball" today simply means any spirit with a sparkling mixer, in the era of the original Holmes and Watson, this would certainly only have been made with Scotch and soda.

2 shots Scotch whisky

3 shots club soda (soda water)

Garnish: lemon zest

Pour ingredients into an ice-filled highball glass and garnish with a large piece of lemon zest submerged in the drink. If you pour in the whisky first, the addition of club soda (soda water) will mix the drink for you, so there's no need to stir.

BAYWATCH

CASEY JEAN "C. J." PARKER | PAMELA ANDERSON

ACTION DRAMA • USA • 1989

Landmark television show *Baywatch*, about lifeguards in Los Angeles and Hawaii, not only inspired thousands of slow-motion beach runs, but also created some of the world's most iconic sex symbols, including C. J. Parker, played by Pamela Anderson. Debuting in 1989, the show dominated 1990s culture, making Anderson a household name along with David Hasselhoff and cast members such as Michael Newman, Alexandra Paul, and Jeremy Jackson.

Joining in season 3, C. J. kickstarted her time on *Baywatch* with a number of gripping storylines, including being deceived into dating a married man and getting caught up in an attempt by thugs to blow up the city pier. Season 4 sees her attempt to rekindle her relationship with ex-boyfriend Cort, support her friend Summer through a severe eating disorder, and fall in love with a man at a sea life park.

1½ shots orange juice

1½ shots cranberry juice

1 shot peach nectar

Garnish: half orange slice and a cocktail cherry

Build the drink in an ice-filled highball glass, stir gently, and garnish.

This twist on the classic Sex on the Beach is a tribute to the sheer sexiness of the *Baywatch* cast, particularly one of its most famous stars, Pamela Anderson.

All that running around in the blistering Malibu sun with little more than a lifesaver and red swimwear could leave you needing serious hydration. Thus, this is a mocktail take on the fruity original, and one that won't disappoint sober guests. Here, the vodka is omitted, and peach schnapps is replaced with peach nectar. If this all sounds too sweet, you can swap out the orange juice with grapefruit juice for a sharper flavor.

FRASIER
FRASIER CRANE | KELSEY GRAMMER
SITCOM • USA • 1993

This sitcom follows Dr. Frasier Crane (played by Kelsey Grammer), a successful therapist who relocates from Boston to Seattle in order to start a new life after his policeman father, Martin, is shot in the hip on duty during a robbery.

Martin struggles with living alone after the incident and moves into Frasier's luxury apartment at the Elliott Bay Towers, along with his dog, Eddie. Daphne Moon, Martin's personal physiotherapist, also moves in. The majority of the show focuses on Frasier adjusting to living with his father, whom he was reluctant to take in in the first place. It becomes apparent that the two had a turbulent past, and they have very little in common now. Frasier spends a lot of time with his younger brother, Niles (played by David Hyde Pierce), a fellow psychiatrist who becomes attracted to Daphne.

Frasier hosts a radio talk show which he uses to share his wit and wisdom, discussing his struggles with his own life, family, and friends with his many listeners.

....

This is a very old cocktail recipe—the Sherry Cobbler even turns up in Charles Dickens' *The Life and Adventures of Martin Chuzzlewit* from 1842. Back then, drinking on ice and through a straw were both novelties. Over the following decades, mixology became widely popularized and the classics entered popular culture.

Frasier and Niles love sherry and always have a decanter on hand, which is intended to be rather quaint and old-fashioned. But the fortified Andalusian wine has surged in popularity in recent years once again, taking it from something only your grandparents drink to a leading cocktail ingredient.

1 lemon wheel

1 orange wheel

¾ shot sugar syrup

3 shots amontillado sherry

Garnish: lots of fruit

In a cocktail shaker, add lemon, orange, and sugar syrup, and muddle. Add sherry and shake with ice. Fine strain into a Collins glass over crushed ice. Top up with additional crushed ice, garnish, and add a straw.

Sidecar

2 shots cognac
¾ shot triple sec
¾ shot fresh lemon juice

Pour all ingredients into a cocktail shaker filled with ice. Shake well and strain into a Martini glass.

BOARDWALK EMPIRE
ENOCH "NUCKY" THOMPSON | STEVE BUSCEMI
PERIOD DRAMA • USA • 2010

Period drama *Boardwalk Empire* is set during Prohibition in the 1920s and '30s. At the center of the show is Enoch "Nucky" Thompson, a political figure who rises to prominence and ultimately takes control of Atlantic City (and is loosely based on real-life politician "Nucky" Johnson).

Nucky, played by Steve Buscemi, is a corrupt Republican politician and crime boss who is portrayed as one of the most powerful people in the USA. Beginning the show as treasurer of Atlantic County, New Jersey, he quickly follows in the footsteps of his predecessor and mentor, Louis Kaestner, the boss of a political and criminal organization that controls every local business.

Although Nucky is unethical, and a part-time gangster, his endearing personality captures the hearts of the Atlantic City people. He's always shaking the right hands and helping charities where he can. His popularity is especially high among the local Irish contingent as well as the African American community, whom he holds influence over through their unofficial leader (and his ally) Chalky White (played by the late Michael K. Williams). This helps Nucky run two successful election campaigns for New Jersey senator Walter Edge, which in turn helps Nucky grow his own political influence.

While the origins of this classic drink aren't certain, its ingredients point to France. The Sidecar became famous thanks to Pat MacGarry, a star bartender of his time who worked at London's Buck's Club in the 1910s. The cocktail then became one of the mainstays at American bars during the early decades of the twentieth century, as depicted in *Boardwalk Empire*.

The original recipe probably called for equal measures of the three ingredients, now known as the "French-style" Sidecar. However, most bars today serve it in the "English style," the style given here, which makes for a balanced tipple in which the cognac has room to shine through.

THE SOPRANOS
TONY SOPRANO | JAMES GANDOLFINI
CRIME DRAMA • USA • 1999

Embroiled in the dark underworld of the New Jersey mob, Tony Soprano seems to have it all: money, family, and power. But behind this intimidating facade lies a broken and tormented man struggling to stay afloat.

Widely regarded as one of the best TV shows of all time, *The Sopranos* centers around the life of Soprano family patriarch Tony (played by the late James Gandolfini). Experiencing a panic attack for the first time after a group of ducks settle in his pool only to fly away, he secretly visits a psychiatrist to address his anxieties.

Outside of the doctor's office, Tony struggles to balance a turbulent home life with his role as a mob boss. Regularly scolded by his hot-headed wife Carmela (Edie Falco), and resented by his children, studious Meadow and troubled A. J., Tony enjoys the power of his position within the Italian American mafia. But with great power comes great responsibility. His business decisions lead to friction with other high-ranking members of the family, rival organizations, and the law—resulting in plots, betrayal, and murder.

1½ shots peaty Scotch whisky

1 shot Chianti red wine

½ shot Drambuie

3 dashes orange bitters

Garnish: flamed orange zest

Add all ingredients to a mixing glass with ice and stir. Strain into a chilled coupe glass and garnish with flamed orange zest. To make this, cut a wide strip of zest from an orange and fold it (orange side out) over the drink to express the oils from orange's skin. Introduce a flame between zest and drink and the oil will ignite en route to the drink's surface, dressing the drink with a bitter orange flavor, and creating a little theater for your guests.

This is a twist on an inventive drink called Mam Knows Best, created by Andrey Kalinin when he was beverage director at Highlands in New York. Its four strong ingredients boast a complex bouquet of flavors all fighting for attention on the palate. But, like any great cocktail, it just works. Here, the shot of Bordeaux in the original recipe is replaced with Tony Soprano's favorite Italian red wine, Chianti. The spiciness and fire will warm even the most frostbitten imbiber.

PARKS AND RECREATION
LESLIE KNOPE | AMY POEHLER
SITCOM • USA • 2009

Parks and Recreation hilariously portrays the absurd, eye-opening antics of an Indiana town's public officials as they work together to make the area a better place for all.

One of the key characters in the sitcom–which unfolds in mockumentary style–is Leslie Knope, played by Amy Poehler. For the vast majority of the show, she serves as the Deputy Director of the Parks and Recreation Department of the fictional city of Pawnee, a role she takes incredibly seriously. Leslie is an over-achiever who firmly believes that the government should always serve the people, and she is dedicated to improving her town. However, her main goal is to ultimately become the first female President of the United States.

In the meantime, idealist Leslie wants to make a beautiful park on the site of a pit that Andy (Chris Pratt) fell into and broke his legs, and so her career improving the civic life of Pawnee goes from strength to strength.

The P&R team will never forget their run-in with the mystery liqueur Snake Juice in season 3 (let's just say it packs quite the punch). All the show's audience knows is that it's coffee-based and contains some other alcoholic ingredients. Thus, the Snake Juice Margarita is essentially the love-child of a Margarita and an Espresso Martini. While this combination might not immediately sound like an obvious recipe for deliciousness, it's a popular mashup with pleasing bittersweet flavors.

1½ shots tequila blanco

¾ shot triple sec

½ shot coffee liqueur

1 shot warm espresso

Rim: sugar

Rim a rocks glass by moistening the rim and dabbing the glass upside down in a saucer of sugar. Fill the glass with ice. Shake all ingredients with ice and strain into the glass.

DOCTOR WHO
DOCTOR WHO | TOM BAKER
SCIENCE FICTION • UK • 1963

Doctor Who chronicles the adventures of an eccentric time-traveling scientist from the remote planet Gallifrey, home of the Time Lords. The Doctor–played by Tom Baker in the fourth regeneration of the series–is a Time Lord who journeys through time and space in his unique craft, the TARDIS (which stands for "Time and Relative Dimension in Space"). The TARDIS is capable of taking on various shapes in order to blend into its environment. While it could transport the Doctor and his passengers anywhere, it's frequently parked on Earth in the form of a blue British police box.

Throughout the show, the Doctor and his colleagues must travel the universe to battle enemies with evil ambitions, such as the Daleks, Cybermen, and other Time Lords. His go-to tool is the Sonic Screwdriver, which uses sonic waves to dismantle or manipulate equipment such as locks and computers.

Over the decades, the series has featured fourteen different Doctors. But Tom Baker served in the role the longest, having played the character from 1974 until 1981.

1 shot vodka

1 shot blue curaçao

5 shots orange juice

2 dashes orange bitters

Garnish: orange zest

Shake all ingredients with ice and strain into an ice-filled Collins glass. Garnish with the largest twist of zest you can peel from an orange, and add a straw.

Cocktails inspired by *Doctor Who* abound, though many are a little too … well, *sci-fi*. So here, the classic Screwdriver has been given a tasty twist to make a colorful but respectable tipple named after a powerful, versatile tool the Doctor uses. Just go easy on the curaçao and test with a quarter shot first, in case the orange juice is already sweet enough. To get that bitter orange bite, be generous with the bitters and express the oil from the zest before twisting and dropping it into the drink.

BUFFY THE VAMPIRE SLAYER
BUFFY SUMMERS | SARAH MICHELLE GELLAR
SUPERNATURAL DRAMA • USA • 1997

Based on a 1992 movie of the same name, *Buffy the Vampire Slayer* revolves around the adventures of its badass titular character. Played by Sarah Michelle Gellar, Buffy Summers is an impressionable teenage girl who is the chosen Slayer of her generation, meaning that she has been tasked by fate to battle vampires, demons, and other supernatural forces of evil. She not only faces the usual daily pressures that come with teenage life, including falling in love (with a vampire), but she also has to stop unholy creatures from taking over the world. Tough gig!

Bringing together distinct elements of drama, horror, and comedy, the show developed a cult following during the 1990s and early 2000s that lives on in internet fandom to this day. Set in the fictional town of Sunnydale, California, and at local school Sunnydale High, *Buffy* is pure escapism at its best, with its witty writing and strong message of female empowerment.

3 shots pineapple juice

½ shot fresh lime juice

Club soda (soda water) to top

1 shot strawberry juice

Garnish: strawberry on a cocktail pick

Shake pineapple and lime juices with ice and strain into an ice-filled Collins glass. Top with soda, float strawberry juice on top, and garnish.

There's only one way to slay a vampire for good, and everyone knows that's a big ol' stake of wood, driven through the heart. In fact, it's probably a pretty effective tactic to use against any mythical monster you wish to dispatch. Here, we celebrate this simple-but-effective move that's kept so many vampire hunters in business over the years. This cocktail presents the impaled organ proudly atop the glass, like a trophy. And of course, since Buffy is still in high school, this is a booze-free concoction that anyone can enjoy.

ABSOLUTELY FABULOUS
PATSY STONE | JOANNA LUMLEY
SITCOM • UK • 1992

One of the most iconic British sitcoms of all time, *Absolutely Fabulous* revolves around high-flying best friends Edina Monsoon (Jennifer Saunders) and Patsy Stone (Joanna Lumley) as they navigate the London fashion scene, hopping from one hedonistic party to the next. Edina's long-suffering daughter Saffron can only roll her eyes from the sidelines, far too sensible to get involved, ultimately playing mother to these two irresponsible delinquents who think they're at the top of their game—but are perhaps not quite as chic as they believe.

Patsy, a stalwart of the swinging '60s, has seen it all. In her opinion, the young, excitable "Cool Britannia" crowd of supermodels, media moguls, and Britpop stars wouldn't know real debauchery if it slapped them in the face. While Edina desperately tries to keep up with whatever the trendsetters are doing, Patsy has a confidence that is both relaxed and inspiringly aloof.

2 drops lavender bitters
1 white sugar cube
1½ shots Stolichnaya vodka
2¼ shots Bollinger Champagne
Garnish: rose petal

Add bitters to the sugar cube and place in a chilled Champagne flute. Pour over Stoli and gently crush the sugar cube. Top with Champagne, stir gently, and garnish.

This unashamedly opulent cocktail is a rare example of one invented within the script of a TV show. But vodka and Champagne together is nothing new—in fact, since the nineteenth century, mixologists have been adding spirits and sugar to bubbly for added flavor and strength.

On the release of the 2016 movie based on *Ab Fab*, the Russian vodka giant Stolichnaya created a number of recipes, including the Stoli-Bolli. The lavender is designed to accentuate the quintessential Englishness of the show, and the floral notes are very welcome in this perfect (and punchy) summer garden-party drink.

THE WIRE

STRINGER BELL | IDRIS ELBA

CRIME DRAMA • USA • 2002

Throwing audiences into the gritty underworld of Baltimore's drug scene, *The Wire* takes a unique look at those on both sides of the law through the eyes of the city's police officers and narcotics dealers, exploring the tragic lives of addicts and the effects on the local community. Over the course of five sprawling seasons, cops and criminals vie for control and try to outsmart each other.

Russell "Stringer" Bell, played by Idris Elba, serves as second-in-command to drug kingpin Avon Barksdale. Stringer's intelligence and business savvy lead him to seek a better way of working. Mercilessly investigated by the Baltimore police department, he has lofty goals of legitimizing the Barksdale empire. Enrolling himself in an economics course at a local community college and distancing himself from the criminal elements of the organization in favor of establishing powerful political connections, Stringer appears to be a model citizen. However, behind closed doors, the reality of the drug scene rears its ugly head, as he is forced to make deadly decisions.

The Wire has come to be known as a brutally realistic look at the American drug trade, and is widely considered to be one of the top television shows of all time.

1½ shots amontillado sherry

½ shot jalapeño-infused tequila blanco

¼ shot Cynar

¾ shot fresh lime juice

½ shot celery juice

½ shot sugar syrup

1 pinch salt

Garnish: celery stick

Shake all ingredients with ice. Strain into an Old Fashioned glass with one large ice cube and garnish.

To make your jalapeño-infused tequila blanco, add one thinly sliced pepper to 2 cups (500 ml) tequila and steep in a mason jar or bottle for 12 hours before straining.

Even the most worldly cocktail connoisseur will struggle to guess the ingredients of this drink. A deep and enigmatic drink is appropriate for a deep and enigmatic man like Stringer. Blending the flavors of Spain, Italy, and Mexico with the juice of limes and celery makes for quite the flavor profile. It's a fine cocktail, reminiscent of a Margarita–but with so many other things going on. This recipe was created by Death & Co., an institution of the Manhattan mixology scene.

IT'S ALWAYS SUNNY IN PHILADELPHIA

CHARLIE KELLY | CHARLIE DAY

SITCOM • USA • 2005

Upon airing a 15th season in late 2021, this popular show became the longest running live-action sitcom in US history. Like many great sitcoms, it follows a peculiar collection of personalities thrown together in a specific location. In this case it's Paddy's Pub in South Philadelphia—an Irish bar that "The Gang" run, each inflicting their idiosyncrasies on the others with hilarious results.

Charles Kelly (played by Charlie Day) is a co-owner at Paddy's, along with partners Mac (Rob McElhenny), Dennis (Glenn Howerton), and Frank (Danny DeVito). He is addicted to a number of different harmful substances such as glue and alcohol, and is known to be illiterate by the other gang members. He's also incredibly interested in the law, and is an easily excitable person who is prone to emotional outbursts. Throughout the show he is noticeably confused by the notions of everyday life, and has anger management issues which often land him in deep trouble.

Yet, despite these problems, Charlie applies himself to his main passions, displaying a natural talent as a pianist and musician. Ultimately, he is the only one of the gang who exhibits any real work ethic.

3 shots milk

2 shots heavy (double) cream

1 dash vanilla extract

⅓ stick cinnamon

1 egg

½ shot sugar syrup

1 shot vodka

1 shot coffee liqueur

½ shot rum or brandy

Garnish: dusting of nutmeg

Warm the milk and cream in a pan with the vanilla and cinnamon. Whisk the egg and sugar syrup together until thick, and then add the warm milk slowly as you whisk. Return the mix to your pan to cook—without boiling—for 4 minutes. Pour into a glass container and leave to cool. Add the alcohol, stir, and refrigerate, preferably overnight. Serve in a Collins glass and garnish.

Ever wondered what crow's eggs, milk, and vodka taste like together? Charlie and Mac's "crowtein" drink for bodyguards called Fight Milk, which they invent in season 8, will satisfy that curiosity!

For good reason it's generally illegal to forage for wild bird eggs, so here, let's stick with whatever your local store has in stock. The result is something akin to a White Russian Eggnog that includes even more protein and a shot of caffeine, thanks to the coffee liqueur. If this doesn't make you fight-ready, nothing will.

LOST

ANA LUCIA CORTEZ | MICHELLE RODRIGUEZ

DRAMA • USA • 2004

The era-defining show *Lost* kicks off when Oceanic Airlines Flight 815 splits in mid-air, and the tail section and fuselage come crashing down on opposite sides of a mysterious island. Ana Lucia Cortez, played by Michelle Rodriguez, ultimately becomes the leader of the tail section of survivors. Her deep-rooted emotional issues quickly come to light as details of her turbulent past are revealed. We learn that, previously, she was the victim of a shooting that killed her unborn child. To get revenge she killed her attacker and subsequently resigned from her role as a police officer in Los Angeles.

In the wake of the plane crash, Ana Lucia only recalls a suitcase hitting her on the head and knocking her out before she woke up in the water and swam to shore. During her time stranded on the island she proves to be quite the hero, giving a child CPR and promising that she will get her home, as well as helping the others to stay out of harm's way.

However, when three members of her group are kidnapped on the island in season 2 and others are attacked a week later, Ana's character really comes to life. Suspecting that there is a spy among them, she becomes the unofficial leader of the tail's passengers, making the decision to help the team to safety.

....

1½ shots Scotch whisky

¾ shot orgeat syrup

½ shot Batavia arrack

1 shot pineapple juice

¾ shot fresh lemon juice

Garnish: pineapple leaves

Blend all ingredients with 1 cup of crushed ice for 5 seconds. Pour into a Tiki mug, fill with more crushed ice, garnish, and add straws.

Tiki-style cocktails are synonymous with rum, the base spirit of choice for most tropical-themed drinks. But given the pivotal role that (fictional) MacCutcheon Scotch whisky plays in *Lost*, a Scotch-based Tiki tipple seems to be the perfect accompaniment for a box-set binge.

This drink was invented by Paul McGee while at Chicago Tiki bar Three Dots and a Dash. The recipe calls for Scotch alongside the popular Southeast Asian spirit arrack, which is not dissimilar to rum, and is one of the oldest known distilled drinks. Overall, this makes for a tropical cocktail with a satisfying depth of flavor.

Tootsie Roll

2 shots Kahlua
4 shots root beer

Pour over ice in a rocks glass, and gently stir.

HOW I MET YOUR MOTHER
SLUTTY PUMPKIN | KATIE HOLMES
SITCOM • USA • 2005

How I Met Your Mother revolves around Ted Mosby (played by Josh Radnor) who, in the year 2030, tells his son and daughter how he met their mom. The show takes place in the past, with "future Ted" recounting tales via voiceover about his youthful times in New York hanging out with his group of pals, including his college best friend Marshall (Jason Segel), Canadian news anchor Robin (Cobie Smulders), womanizer Barney (Neil Patrick Harris), and kindergarten teacher Lily (Alyson Hannigan).

In season 1, Ted recounts to his kids how, four years earlier, he met an attractive woman he nicknamed the "Slutty Pumpkin" at a rooftop Halloween party, but regrettably lost the KitKat wrapper she had written her number on. Ted, who loves Halloween, describes waiting patiently for her to appear again each year. Eventually, he spots the titillating outfit in the window of a costume shop, and goes out of his way to find out the name of the woman who rented it.

He finally meets Naomi, the Slutty Pumpkin (played by Katie Holmes), only to realize that they have no chemistry whatsoever. Despite this, Ted struggles to cut contact, falling in love with her all over again upon seeing her in that outfit on the rooftop, both wearing the same costumes as they did on the night when they first met.

....

This very simple cocktail is the drink of choice for the Slutty Pumpkin, and one that is guaranteed to divide opinion at any cocktail party. There are two sources of debate: Does it taste like its candy namesake? And, is it even a good drink?

On the first question, despite the absence of chocolate, there is an uncanny similarity in flavor with the much-loved candy. But there are other notes in there that will throw some people off. And so, on to the second point: Is this a good drink at all? Well, you do have to like root beer, which is an acquired taste (especially outside of the USA).

HAPPY DAYS
ARTHUR "FONZIE" FONZARELLI | HENRY WINKLER
SITCOM • USA • 1974

Widely recognized as one of the most iconic TV shows of the 1970s, *Happy Days* centers around the experiences and dilemmas of innocent teenager Richie Cunningham (Ron Howard). The epitome of an all-American 1950s boy, Richie sometimes gets himself into trouble, usually due to his attempts to attract women. (And when he's feeling lucky with the ladies, he sings "I found my thrill, on Blueberry Hill" in the style of Fats Domino.)

While Richie is undoubtedly the star of *Happy Days* initially, over the seasons he becomes overshadowed by Arthur Herbert Fonzarelli, better known as "Fonzie" or "The Fonz," played by Henry Winkler. The embodiment of slick and cool, he fits the "greaser" stereotype of the confident, leather-clad motorcyclist. But, much like later TV characters he set the template for (such as Joey from Friends), Fonzie's vanity and simple nature become the source of laughs—and affection for the character.

2 shots stout beer

1 shot spiced rum

½ shot dark crème de cacao liqueur

2 scoops vanilla ice cream

1 tablespoon chocolate syrup

1 tablespoon salted caramel syrup

Garnish: whipped cream and a drizzle of both syrups

Blend all ingredients until smooth, pour into a Collins glass, and garnish.

One of the Hard Rock Café's signature cocktails, the Twist and Shout, is a decadent hard shake. Popular across the iconic music-themed restaurant's global empire, it's the ultimate grown-up take on an American diner milkshake.

Rum, chocolate, and stout beget a great combination of flavors that never fails to please. If you're stuck for dark crème de cacao you can use any chocolate liqueur, though if it's not specifically dark you'll lose that depth and bitterness. In a pinch, you can use an extra spoonful of chocolate syrup or even Kahlua.

BROAD CITY
ILANA WEXLER AND ABBI ABRAMS | ILANA GLAZER AND ABBI JACOBSON
SITCOM • USA • 2014

Broad City follows two young women as they navigate their daily lives in New York City, enjoying the rollercoaster of twenty-something life with all its highs, lows, and randomness.

Both in their twenties, Ilana Wexler (played by Ilana Glazer) and Abbi Abrams (Abbi Jacobson) have the world at their feet and live wild, carefree lives. Throughout the show, Ilana tries to avoid working as much as possible, while Abbi wants to forge a career as an artist. But Abbi's current role is cleaning at high-end fitness studio Soulstice, where she's constantly called upon to resolve gross-sounding emergencies in the changing rooms. If only she could rise to becoming a fitness instructor, let alone a world-renowned artist.

Ilana is an idealist, working her sales job at a coupon deals company while constantly rebelling against the corporate machine and capitalism in general. She'd rather stay home smoking weed and cooking up crazy plans, beat the city streets in search of adventure, or just hang out with her boyfriend of convenience, dentist Lincoln (Hannibal Buress).

1½ shots tequila blanco

½ shot triple sec

¾ shot fresh lime juice

4 hulled strawberries

1 shot Hennessy cognac, for the test tube

Garnish: lime wedge

Blend first 4 ingredients with 6 shots of crushed ice and pour into a chilled Margarita glass. Place a test tube containing Hennessy in the ice and garnish with a lime wedge on the rim, an umbrella, and a straw.

It's the girls' "Friendiversary," and Ilana has led Abbi on a long, complex scavenger hunt across the city before they finally arrive at their favorite eatery–Houston BBQ–each clutching a huge cardboard cut-out of the other's head. The frozen cocktails are already served, and the huge plates of chicken wings are on their way (along with the anticipation of digestive issues expected after the gargantuan feast). As is common in casual themed restaurants of this type, the cocktails are "upgraded" with "Henny" shots in test tubes, which serve as a chaser to get the party started.

NEW GIRL
WINSTON BISHOP | LAMORNE MORRIS
SITCOM • USA • 2011

The *New Girl* of the title is Jessica Day, a schoolteacher, played by Zooey Deschanel. This fun and energetic sitcom follows Jess' life in Los Angeles after she catches her boyfriend cheating and moves into a loft with three men: Nick Miller, Winston Schmidt, and Winston Bishop.

The latter Winston (played by Lamorne Morris) grew up in Chicago with his best friend and current roommate Nick. Incredibly talented, he excelled at basketball and made it all the way to the pros, often stating, "I was the ninth guy off the bench for the eighth-best team in Latvia." However, after returning from playing overseas, he finds himself unemployed, with few skills and a resume that fails to impress.

Oblivious and goofy, Winston's endearing personality is what makes this character so infectious–especially when it comes to pranking people, spouting bad opening lines when trying to hit on girls, and displaying childlike qualities.

....

Winston loves fruity drinks, and The Weirdness is his favorite. It's everything you'd want from a Tiki-style cocktail: rum, juice, and orgeat syrup (an almond-infused syrup common in this type of drink, most famously the Mai Tai).

It's a visual feast too, preferably served up in a young coconut shell (the soft white type), though a hard shell or even a Tiki mug will do fine too. The key to really nailing this drink, though, is the garnish. Go big and flamboyant, with tropical fruits and edible flowers (violets, pansies, roses, hibiscus, daisies, and marigolds are good choices).

1½ shots aged rum

¾ shot cognac

2 shots orange juice

1 shot fresh lemon juice

½ shot orgeat syrup

Garnish: fruit skewer and edible flowers

Blend all ingredients with ¾ cup crushed ice, pour into a hollowed-out coconut shell, garnish, and add a bendy straw and an umbrella.

THE WALKING DEAD
MICHONNE HAWTHORNE | DANAI GURIRA
HORROR • USA • 2010

When Deputy Rick Grimes (Andrew Lincoln) is shot in the shoulder while on police duty, he falls into a coma–and wakes up only to find himself in the middle of a zombie apocalypse. He then sets out on a mission to locate his family and protect them. A natural leader, Rick acquires a team of fellow survivors who look to him for guidance and protection from the "walkers." Over the course of 11 seasons, *The Walking Dead* follows this unlikely group as they seek to rebuild their world, and chronicles the struggles and moments of joy they have along the way.

Played by Danai Gurira, Michonne Hawthorne is one of the show's central characters; she's a tough but good-hearted survivor who prides herself on her ability to work alone. Having lost her toddler in the initial outbreak, Michonne withdrew into solitude, focusing on developing her sword skills and becoming a ruthless warrior.

When we first meet Michonne, she is travelling with two armless, jawless walkers whom she uses to carry supplies and fend off attackers. She comes across Rick and the rest of the survivors when she leaves Woodbury, a new township ruled by the deceitful "Governor." Although determined to stay independent, Michonne bonds with Rick's son Carl and eventually becomes a core member of the group. She retains her suspicion of outsiders, however, and finds it difficult to trust newcomers.

1½ shots golden rum
1 shot dark rum
½ shot white rum
½ shot apricot liqueur
1 shot fresh lime juice
¾ shot pineapple juice
½ shot sugar syrup
½ shot 151-proof rum

Garnish: pineapple slice

Shake all ingredients except the 151-proof rum with ice. Strain into a Hurricane glass filled with crushed ice. Float the overproof rum over the top (which can be set alight should you desire some theater in your presentation), and garnish.

One of many drinks invented by mixologist Donn Beach, the Zombie is a Tiki classic. Like so many cocktails invented during the explosion of South Pacific influences on mid-century culture, it's rum-based, and in this case contains four different kinds.

The Zombie is notable, and probably so-called, for its high alcohol content. It's certainly not a drink to be taken lightly (Donn would only serve you two of these in one night!). While the last ingredient–151-proof rum–might seem excessive, in reality this is mostly burnt off thanks to the flaming serve.

Acknowledgments

Thanks to Ali, Martha, and the team at Prestel for all your hard work.

Most of all, thanks to
Sonny and Hugh
for putting up with such busy parents
during endeavors like this.

About the Authors

Will Francis educates professionals from the world's leading brands on digital technology and creativity through his lectures and workshops. He also appears in the media to share his expertise on these topics. He is the co-author of *Cocktails of the Movies*. His favorite TV show is *Mad Men*, served with an Old Fashioned.

Stacey Marsh is a digital designer and illustrator who has worked with some of the world's most loved brands. She is Head of Design at product design agency Fathom London, where she creates user interfaces for technology and finance clients. She is the co-author of *Cocktails of the Movies*. Her favorite show is *The Office* (US), and a French 75 is her perfect tipple.

© Prestel Verlag, Munich · London · New York, 2023

A member of Penguin Random House Verlagsgruppe GmbH
Neumarkter Strasse 28 · 81673 Munich

© for the text by Will Francis, 2023
© for the illustrations by Stacey Marsh, 2023

Library of Congress Control Number: 2022951611

A CIP catalogue record for this book is available from the British Library.

Editorial direction: Ali Gitlow
Copyediting and proofreading: Martha Jay
Design and layout: Stacey Marsh
Production management: Luisa Klose
Separations: Reproline Mediateam, Munich
Printing and binding: Livonia Print, Riga
Paper: Magno Volume

Penguin Random House Verlagsgruppe FSC® N001967

Printed in Latvia

ISBN 978-3-7913-8822-9

www.prestel.com